Contents

Introduction 2
The game 3
The Laws of Cricket 4
  The Preamble – The Spirit of Cricket 4
  The players 5
  Substitutes and runners; batsman or
    fielder leaving the field; batsman
    retiring; batsman commencing
    innings 5
  The umpires 7
  The scorers 11
  The ball 12
  The bat 13
  The pitch 13
  The wickets 13
  The bowling, popping
    and return creases 15
  Preparation and maintenance
    of the playing area 16
  Covering the pitch 17
  Innings 18
  The follow-on 18
  Declaration and forfeiture 19
  Intervals 19
  Start of play; cessation of play 21
  Practice on the field 23

Scoring runs 23
Boundaries 25
Lost ball 27
The result 27
The over 29
Dead ball 30
No ball 31
Wide ball 34
Bye and Leg bye 34
Appeals 35
The wicket is down 37
Batsman out of his ground 37
Bowled 38
Timed out 38
Caught 39
Handled the ball 40
Hit the ball twice 40
Hit wicket 41
Leg before wicket 43
Obstructing the field 44
Run out 44
Stumped 45
The wicket-keeper 46
The fielder 47
Fair and unfair play 49
Index 56

Acknowledgements
The publishers would like to thank
Gray-Nicolls for their photographic
contribution to this book.

All photographs courtesy of Empics.
Illustrations by Tim Bairstow of Taurus
Graphics.

Note The players, umpires and scorers
in a game of cricket may be of either
gender and the Laws apply equally to
both. The use, throughout the text, of
pronouns indicating the male gender is
purely for brevity. Except where specifically stated otherwise, every provision
of the Laws is to be read as applying to
women and girls equally as to men and
boys.

Introduction

The game of Cricket has been governed by a series of Codes of Law for over 250 years. These Codes have been subject to additions and alterations recommended by the governing authorities of the time. Since its formation in 1787, the Marylebone Cricket Club (MCC) has been recognised as the sole authority for drawing up the Code and for all subsequent amendments. The Club also holds the World copyright.

The basic Laws of Cricket have stood remarkably well the test of over 250 years of playing the game. It is thought the real reason for this is that cricketers have traditionally been prepared to play in the Spirit of the Game as well as in accordance with the Laws.

In 2000, MCC revised and re-wrote the Laws for the new Millennium. In this Code, the major innovation is the introduction of the Spirit of Cricket as a Preamble to the Laws. Whereas in the past it was assumed that the implicit Spirit of the Game was understood and accepted by all those involved, MCC felt it right to put into words some clear guidelines, which help to maintain the unique character and enjoyment of the game. The other aims were to dispense with the Notes, to incorporate all the points into the Laws and to remove, where possible, any ambiguities, so that captains, players and umpires could continue to enjoy the game at whatever level they might be playing. MCC consulted widely with all the Full Member Countries of the International Cricket Council, the Governing Body of the game. There was close consultation with the Association of Cricket Umpires and Scorers. The Club also brought in umpires and players from all round the world.

The latest version, The Laws of Cricket (2000 Code 2nd Edition – 2003) includes several necessary amendments arising from experience and practical application of the Code around the world since 2000. Sections of the Laws have been picked out in red; these represent those which have been most extensively revised.

R D V Knight
Secretary & Chief Executive MCC
Lord's Cricket Ground
London NW8 8QN

May 2003

The game

Cricket is played between two teams, normally 11 a side, and gives the maximum opportunity for combining team effort with individual skill and initiative. Each team bats, or takes its innings, in turn – the choice for first innings being decided by toss. The game is played on a pitch on which two wickets are placed 22 yards (20.12 m) apart, although this distance may be reduced for children.

The two batsmen defend these wickets against the bowling of the fielding side, and when a batsman is 'out' his place is taken by another, and so on until ten batsmen are out or until the innings has been declared closed.

A bowler from the fielding side bowls an over of 6 balls from one end to the opposite batsman defending his wicket, and aims to dismiss him in one of the ways provided for in the Laws.

The more common methods of dismissing a batsman are the bowling down of the striker's wicket, catching him from a stroke, his being Leg before wicket, stumping by the wicket-keeper when he has gone out of his ground, and by either batsman being run out.

Overs are bowled successively from alternate ends. No bowler can bowl two overs in succession, but otherwise the captain of the fielding side can change his bowling as he thinks fit.

The score is reckoned by 'runs', i.e. the number of times the batsmen run from end to end of the area between the 'popping crease' at each end of the pitch. Runs are usually the result of hits, but can be scored when the ball has not actually been hit by the striker, e.g. 'Byes' and 'Leg byes', or as penalties for 'Wides' and 'No balls'. The fielding side has the twofold object of dismissing the opposing batsmen and of preventing them from scoring runs.

When the first side has completed its innings, the other side starts its own. A match may consist of one or two innings by each side. The side scoring the largest aggregate of runs in the match wins. If the match is not played out to a finish, it is regarded as drawn.

The Laws of Cricket

The Preamble – The Spirit of Cricket

Cricket is a game that owes much of its unique appeal to the fact that it should be played not only within its Laws but also within the Spirit of the Game. Any action which is seen to abuse this spirit causes injury to the game itself. The major responsibility for ensuring the spirit of fair play rests with the captains.

1. There are two Laws which place the responsibility for the team's conduct firmly on the captain.

Responsibility of captains

The captains are responsible at all times for ensuring that play is conducted within the Spirit of the Game as well as within the Laws.

Player's conduct

In the event of a player failing to comply with instructions by an umpire, or criticising by word or action the decisions of an umpire, or showing dissent, or generally behaving in a manner which might bring the game into disrepute, the umpire concerned shall in the first place report the matter to the other umpire and to the player's captain, and instruct the latter to take action.

2. Fair and unfair play

According to the Laws the umpires are the sole judges of fair and unfair play.
The umpires may intervene at any time and it is the responsibility of the captain to take action where required.

3. The umpires are authorised to intervene in cases of:
- Time wasting
- Damaging the pitch
- Dangerous or unfair bowling
- Tampering with the ball
- Any other action that they consider to be unfair

4. The Spirit of the Game involves RESPECT **for:**
- Your opponents
- Your own captain and team
- The role of the umpires
- The game's traditional values

5. It is against the Spirit of the Game:
- To dispute an umpire's decision by word, action or gesture
- To direct abusive language towards an opponent or umpire
- To indulge in cheating or any sharp practice, for instance:

a to appeal knowing that the batsman is not out

b to advance towards an umpire in an aggressive manner when appealing

c to seek to distract an opponent either verbally or by harassment with persistent clapping or unnecessary noise under the guise of enthusiasm and motivation of one's own side

6. Violence

There is no place for any act of violence on the field of play.

7. Players

Captains and umpires together set the tone for the conduct of a cricket match. Every player is expected to make an important contribution to this.

Law 1 – the players

1. Number of players

A match is played between two sides, each of eleven players, one of whom shall be captain. By agreement a match may be played between sides of more or less than eleven players, but not more than eleven players may field at any time.

2. Nomination of players

Each captain shall nominate his players in writing to one of the umpires before the toss. No player may be changed after the nomination without the consent of the opposing captain.

3. Captain

If at any time the captain is not available, a deputy shall act for him.
a If a captain is not available during the period in which the toss is to take place, then the deputy must be responsible for the nomination of the players, if this has not already been done, and for the toss. *See* **2** above and Law 12.4 (The toss).
b At any time after the toss, the deputy must be one of the nominated players.

4. Responsibility of captains

The captains are responsible at all times for ensuring that play is conducted within the spirit and traditions of the game as well as within the Laws. *See* The Preamble – The Spirit of Cricket and Law 42.1 (Fair and unfair play – responsibility of captains).

Law 2 – substitutes and runners; batsman or fielder leaving the field; batsman retiring; batsman commencing innings

1. Substitutes and runners

a If the umpires are satisfied that a player has been injured or become ill after the nomination of the players, they shall allow that player to have:
(i) a substitute acting instead of him in the field
(ii) a runner when batting.
Any injury or illness that occurs at any time after the nomination of the players until the conclusion of the match shall be allowable, irrespective of whether play is in progress or not.
b The umpires shall have discretion, for other wholly acceptable reasons, to allow a

substitute for a fielder, or a runner for a batsman, at the start of the match or at any subsequent time.

c A player wishing to change his shirt, boots, etc. must leave the field to do so. No substitute shall be allowed for him.

2. Objection to substitutes

The opposing captain shall have no right of objection to any player acting as a substitute on the field, nor as to where the substitute shall field. However, no substitute shall act as wicket-keeper. *See* **3** below.

3. Restrictions on the role of substitutes

A substitute shall not be allowed to bat or bowl nor to act as wicket-keeper or as captain on the field of play.

4. A player for whom a substitute has acted

A player is allowed to bat, bowl or field even though a substitute has previously acted for him.

5. Fielder absent or leaving the field

If a fielder fails to take the field with his side at the start of the match or at any later time, or leaves the field during a session of play:

a the umpire shall be informed of the reason for his absence

b he shall not thereafter come on to the field during a session of play without the consent of the umpire. *See* **6** below. The umpire shall give such consent as soon as is practicable.

c If he is absent for 15 minutes or longer, he shall not be permitted to bowl thereafter, subject to (i), (ii) or (iii) below, until he has been on the field for at least that length of playing time for which he was absent.

(i) Absence or penalty for time absent shall not be carried over into a new day's play.

(ii) If, in the case of a follow-on or forfeiture, a side fields for two consecutive innings, this restriction shall, subject to (i) above, continue as necessary into the second innings but shall not otherwise be carried over into a new innings.

(iii) The time lost for an unscheduled break in play shall be counted as time on the field for any fielder who comes on to the field at the resumption of play. *See* Law 15.1 (An interval).

6. Player returning without permission

If a player comes on to the field of play in contravention of **5b** above and comes into contact with the ball while it is in play:

(i) the ball shall immediately become dead and the umpire shall award 5 penalty runs

to the batting side. *See* Law 42.17 (Penalty runs). The ball shall not count as one of the over.

(ii) the umpire shall inform the other umpire, the captain of the fielding side, the batsmen and, as soon as practicable, the captain of the batting side of the reason for this action

(iii) the umpires together shall report the occurrence as soon as possible to the Executive of the fielding side and any Governing Body responsible for the match, who shall take such action as is considered appropriate against the captain and player concerned.

7. Runner

The player acting as a runner for a batsman shall be a member of the batting side and shall, if possible, have already batted in that innings. The runner shall wear external protective equipment equivalent to that worn by the batsman for whom he runs and shall carry a bat.

8. Transgression of the Laws by a batsman who has a runner

a A batsman's runner is subject to the Laws. He will be regarded as a batsman except where there are specific provisions for his role as a runner. *See* **7** above and Law 29.2 (Which is a batsman's ground).

b A batsman with a runner will suffer the penalty for any infringement of the Laws by his runner as though he had been himself responsible for the infringement. In particular he will be out if his runner is out under any of Laws 33 (Handled the ball), 37 (Obstructing the field) or 38 (Run out).
c When a batsman with a runner is striker he remains himself subject to the Laws and will be liable to the penalties that any infringement of them demands.

Additionally, if he is out of his ground when the wicket is put down at the wicket-keeper's end, he will be out in the circumstances of Law 38 (Run out) or Law 39 (Stumped) irrespective of the position of the non-striker or of the runner. If he is thus dismissed, runs completed by the runner and the other batsman before the dismissal shall not be scored. However, the penalty for a No ball or a Wide shall stand, together with any penalties to either side that may be awarded when the ball is dead. *See* Law 42.17 (Penalty runs).
d When a batsman with a runner is not the striker:
(i) he remains subject to Laws 33 (Handled the ball) and 37 (Obstructing the field) but is otherwise out of the game

(ii) he shall stand where directed by the striker's end umpire so as not to interfere with play
(iii) he will be liable, notwithstanding (i) above, to the penalty demanded by the Laws should he commit any act of unfair play.

9. Batsman leaving the field or retiring
A batsman may retire at any time during his innings. The umpires, before allowing play to proceed, shall be informed of the reason for a batsman retiring.
a If a batsman retires because of illness, injury or any other unavoidable cause, he is entitled to resume his innings subject to **c** below. If for any reason he does not do so, his innings is to be recorded as 'Retired – not out'.
b If a batsman retires for any reason other than as in **a** above, he may only resume his innings with the consent of the opposing captain. If for any reason he does not resume his innings it is to be recorded as 'Retired – out'.
c If after retiring a batsman resumes his innings, it shall be only at the fall of a wicket or the retirement of another batsman.

10. Commencement of a batsman's innings
Except at the start of a side's innings, a batsman shall be considered to have commenced his innings when he first steps on to the field of play, provided Time has not been called. The innings of the opening batsmen, and that of any new batsman at the resumption of play after a call of Time, shall commence at the call of Play.

Law 3 – the umpires

1. Appointment and attendance
Before the match, two umpires shall be appointed, one for each end, to control the game as required by the Laws, with absolute impartiality. The umpires shall be present on the ground and report to the Executive of the ground at least 45 minutes before the scheduled start of each day's play.

2. Change of umpire
An umpire shall not be changed during the match, other than in exceptional circumstances, unless he is injured or ill. If there has to be a change of umpire, the replacement shall act only as the striker's end umpire unless the captains agree that he should take full responsibility as an umpire.

3. Agreement with captains

Before the toss the umpires shall:

a ascertain the hours of play and agree with the captains

(i) the balls to be used during the match. *See* Law 5 (The ball)

(ii) times and durations of intervals for meals and times for drinks intervals. *See* Law 15 (Intervals)

(iii) the boundary of the field of play and allowances for boundaries. *See* Law 19 (Boundaries)

(iv) any special conditions of play affecting the conduct of the match.

b inform the scorers of the agreements in (ii), (iii) and (iv) above.

4. To inform captains and scorers

Before the toss the umpires shall agree between themselves and inform both captains and both scorers:

(i) which clock or watch and back-up time piece is to be used during the match

(ii) whether or not any obstacle within the field of play is to be regarded as a boundary. *See* Law 19 (Boundaries).

5. The wickets, creases and boundaries

Before the toss and during the match, the umpires shall satisfy themselves that:

(i) the wickets are properly pitched. *See* Law 8 (The wickets)

(ii) the creases are correctly marked. *See* Law 9 (The bowling, popping and return creases)

(iii) the boundary of the field of play complies with the requirements of Law 19.2 (Defining the boundary – boundary marking).

6. Conduct of the game, implements and equipment

Before the toss and during the match, the umpires shall satisfy themselves that:

a the conduct of the game is strictly in accordance with the Laws

b the implements of the game conform to the requirements of Laws 5 (The ball) and 6 (The bat), together with either Laws 8.2 (Size of stumps) and 8.3 (The bails) or, if appropriate, Law 8.4 (Junior cricket)

c (i) no player uses equipment other than that permitted

(ii) the wicket-keeper's gloves comply with the requirements of Law 40.2 (Gloves). *See* fig. 6.

7. Fair and unfair play

The umpires shall be the sole judges of fair and unfair play.

8. Fitness of ground, weather and light

The umpires shall be the final judges of the fitness of the ground, weather and light for play. *See* **9** below and Law 7.2 (Fitness of the pitch for play).

9. Suspension of play for adverse conditions of ground, weather or light

a (i) All references to ground include the pitch. *See* Law 7.1 (Area of pitch).

(ii) For the purpose of this Law and Law 15.9**b** (ii) (Intervals for drinks) only, the batsmen at the wicket may deputise for their captain at any appropriate time.

b If at any time the umpires together agree that the condition of the ground, weather or light is not suitable for play, they shall inform the captains and, unless

(i) in unsuitable ground or weather conditions both captains agree to continue, or to commence, or to restart play, or

(ii) in unsuitable light the batting side wish to continue, or to commence, or to restart play,

they shall suspend play, or not allow play to commence or to restart.

c (i) After agreeing to play in unsuitable ground or weather conditions, either captain may appeal against the conditions to the umpires before the next call of Time. The umpires shall uphold the appeal only if, in their opinion, the factors taken into account when making their previous decision are the same or the conditions have further deteriorated.

(ii) After deciding to play in unsuitable light, the captain of the batting side may appeal against the light to the umpires before the next call of Time. The umpires shall uphold the appeal only if, in their opinion, the factors taken into account when making their previous decision are the same or the condition of the light has further deteriorated.

d If at any time the umpires together agree that the conditions of ground, weather or light are so bad that there is obvious and foreseeable risk to the safety of any player or umpire, so that it would be unreasonable or dangerous for play to take place, then notwithstanding the provisions of **b** (i) and **b** (ii) above, they shall immediately suspend play, or not allow play to commence or to restart. The decision as to whether conditions are so bad as to warrant such action is one for the umpires alone to make.

The fact that the grass and the ball are wet and slippery does not warrant the ground conditions being regarded as unreasonable or dangerous. If the umpires consider the ground is so wet or slippery as to deprive the bowler of a reasonable foothold, the fielders of the power of free movement, or the batsmen of the ability to play their strokes or to run between the wickets, then these conditions shall be regarded as so bad that it would be unreasonable for play to take place.

e When there is a suspension of play it is the responsibility of the umpires to monitor the conditions. They shall make inspections as often as appropriate, unaccompanied by any of the players or officials. Immediately the umpires together agree that conditions are suitable for play they shall call upon the players to resume the game.

f If play is in progress up to the start of an agreed interval then it will resume after the interval unless the umpires together agree that conditions are or have become unsuitable or dangerous. If they do so agree, then they shall implement the procedure in **b** or **d** above, as appropriate, whether or not there had been any decision by the captains to continue, or any appeal against the conditions by either captain, prior to the commencement of the interval.

10. Exceptional circumstances

The umpires shall have the discretion to implement the procedures of **9** above for reasons other than ground, weather or light if they consider that exceptional circumstances warrant it.

11. Position of umpires

The umpires shall stand where they can best see any act upon which their decision may be required.

Subject to this over-riding consideration the umpire at the bowler's end shall stand where he does not interfere with either the bowler's run up or the striker's view.

The umpire at the striker's end may elect to stand on the off side instead of the on side of the pitch, provided he informs the captain of the fielding side, the striker and the other umpire of his intention to do so.

12. Umpires changing ends

The umpires shall change ends after each side has had one completed innings. *See* Law 14.2 (Forfeiture of an innings).

13. Consultation between umpires

All disputes shall be determined by the umpires. The umpires shall consult with each other whenever necessary. *See* also Law 27.6 (Consultation by umpires).

Signals made while the ball is in play.

Dead ball – by crossing and re-crossing the wrists below the waist.
No ball – by extending one arm horizontally.
Out – by raising an index finger above the head. (If not out the umpire shall call Not out.)
Wide – by extending both arms horizontally.

When the ball is dead, the signals above, with the exception of the signal for Out, shall be repeated to the scorers. The signals listed below shall be made to the scorers only when the ball is dead.

Boundary 4 – by waving an arm from side to side finishing with the arm across the chest.
Boundary 6 – by raising both arms above the head.
Bye – by raising an open hand above the head.
Commencement of last hour – by pointing to a raised wrist with the other hand.
Five penalty runs awarded to the batting side – by repeated tapping of one shoulder with the opposite hand.
Five penalty runs awarded to the fielding side – by placing one hand on the opposite shoulder.
Leg bye – by touching a raised knee with the hand.
New ball – by holding the ball above the head.
Revoke last signal – by touching both shoulders, each with the opposite hand.
Short run – by bending one arm upwards and touching the nearer shoulder with the tips of the fingers.

14. Signals
a The code of signals on page 10 shall be used by umpires.
b The umpires shall wait until each signal to the scorers has been separately acknowledged by a scorer before allowing play to proceed.

15. Correctness of scores
Consultation between umpires and scorers on doubtful points is essential. The umpires shall satisfy themselves as to the correctness of the number of runs scored, the wickets that have fallen and, where appropriate, the number of overs bowled. They shall agree these with the scorers at least at every interval, other than a drinks interval, and at the conclusion of the match. *See* Laws 4.2 (Correctness of scores), 21.8 (Correctness of result) and 21.10 (Result not to be changed).

Law 4 – the scorers

1. Appointment of scorers

Two scorers shall be appointed to record all runs scored, all wickets taken and, where appropriate, number of overs bowled.

2. Correctness of scores

The scorers shall frequently check to ensure that their records agree. They shall agree with the umpires, at least at every interval, other than a drinks interval, and at the conclusion of the match, the runs scored, the wickets that have fallen and, where appropriate, the number of overs bowled. *See* Law 3.15 (Correctness of scores).

3. Acknowledging signals

The scorers shall accept all instructions and signals given to them by the umpires. They shall immediately acknowledge each separate signal.

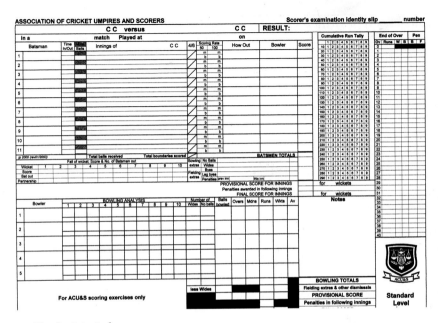

▲ *Fig. 1 A typical score sheet and bowling analysis*

Law 5 – the ball

1. Weight and size

The ball, when new, shall weigh not less than 5½ ounces/155.9 g, nor more than 5¾ ounces/163 g, and shall measure not less than $8^{13}/_{16}$ in/22.4 cm, nor more than 9 in/22.9 cm in circumference.

2. Approval and control of balls

a All balls to be used in the match, having been approved by the umpires and captains, shall be in the possession of the umpires before the toss and shall remain under their control throughout the match.

b The umpire shall take possession of the ball in use at the fall of each wicket, at the start of any interval and at any interruption of play.

3. New ball

Unless an agreement to the contrary has been made before the match, either captain may demand a new ball at the start of each innings.

4. New ball in match of more than one day's duration

In a match of more than one day's duration, the captain of the fielding side may demand a new ball after the prescribed number of overs has been bowled with the old one. The Governing Body for cricket in the country concerned shall decide the number of overs applicable in that country, which shall not be less than 75 overs.

The umpires shall indicate to the batsmen and the scorers whenever a new ball is taken into play.

5. Ball lost or becoming unfit for play

If, during play, the ball cannot be found or recovered or the umpires agree that it has become unfit for play through normal use, the umpires shall replace it with a ball which has had wear comparable with that which the previous ball had received before the need for its replacement. When the ball is replaced the umpires shall inform the batsmen and the fielding captain.

6. Specifications

The specifications as described in **1** above shall apply to men's cricket only. The following specifications will apply to:

(i) Women
Weight: from $4^{15}/_{16}$ ounces/140 g to $5^{5}/_{16}$ ounces/151 g; Circumference: from 8¼ in/21.0 cm to 8⅞ in/22.5 cm

(ii) Junior (under 13)
Weight: from $4^{11}/_{16}$ ounces/133 g to $5^{1}/_{16}$ ounces/144 g; Circumference: from $8^{1}/_{16}$ in/20.5cm to $8^{11}/_{16}$ in/22.0 cm.

Law 6 – The bat

1. Width and length
The bat overall shall not be more than 38 in/96.5 cm in length. The blade of the bat shall be made solely of wood and shall not exceed 4¼ in/10.8 cm at the widest part.

2. Covering the blade
The blade may be covered with material for protection, strengthening or repair. Such material shall not exceed ¹/₁₆ in/1.56 mm in thickness, and shall not be likely to cause unacceptable damage to the ball.

3. Hand or glove to count as part of bat
In these Laws:
a reference to the bat shall imply that the bat is held by the batsman
b contact between the ball and, either
(i) the striker's bat itself, or
(ii) the striker's hand holding the bat, or
(iii) any part of a glove worn on the striker's hand holding the bat
shall be regarded as the ball striking or touching the bat, or being struck by the bat.

The following are to be considered as part of the bat:

- the whole of the bat itself
- the whole of a glove (or gloves) worn on a hand (or hands) holding the bat
- the hand (or hands) holding the bat, if the batsman is not wearing a glove on that hand or on those hands.

Law 7 – the pitch

1. Area of pitch
The pitch is a rectangular area of the ground 22 yds/20.12 m in length and 10 ft/3.05 m in width. It is bounded at either end by the bowling creases and on either side by imaginary lines, one each side of the imaginary line joining the centres of the two middle stumps, each parallel to it and 5 ft/1.52 m from it. *See* Laws 8.1 (Width and pitching) and 9.2 (The bowling crease).

2. Fitness of the pitch for play
The umpires shall be the final judges of the fitness of the pitch for play. *See* Laws 3.8 (Fitness of ground, weather and light) and 3.9 (Suspension of play for adverse conditions of ground, weather or light).

3. Selection and preparation
Before the match, the Ground Authority shall be responsible for the selection and preparation of the pitch. During the match, the umpires shall control its use and maintenance.

4. Changing the pitch
The pitch shall not be changed during the match unless the umpires decide that it is unreasonable or dangerous for play to continue on it and then only with the consent of both captains.

5. Non-turf pitches
In the event of a non-turf pitch being used, the artificial surface shall conform to the following measurements:

Length – a minimum of 58 ft/17.68 m
Width – a minimum of 6 ft/1.83 m

See Law 10.8 (Non-turf pitches).

Law 8 – the wickets

1. Width and pitching
Two sets of wickets shall be pitched opposite and parallel to each other at a distance of 22 yds/20.12 m between the centres of the two middle stumps. Each set shall be

9 in/22.86 cm wide and shall consist of three wooden stumps with two wooden bails on top. *See* fig. 2.

2. Size of stumps
The tops of the stumps shall be 28 in/71.1 cm above the playing surface and shall be dome shaped except for the bail grooves. The portion of a stump above the playing surface shall be cylindrical, apart from the domed top, with circular section of diameter not less than 1⅜ in/3.49 cm nor more than 1½ in/3.81 cm. *See* fig. 2.

3. The bails
a The bails, when in position on the top of the stumps:
(i) shall not project more than ½ in/1.27 cm above them
(ii) shall fit between the stumps without forcing them out of the vertical.
b Each bail shall conform to the following specifications. *See* fig. 2.

Overall length – 4⁵/₁₆ in/10.95 cm
Barrel length – 2⅛ in/5.40 cm
Longer spigot – 1⅜ in/3.49 cm
Shorter spigot – 1³/₁₆ in/2.06 cm

4. Junior cricket
In junior cricket, the same definitions of the wickets shall apply subject to following measurements being used:

Width – 8 in/20.32 cm
Pitched for under 13 – 21 yds/19.20 m
Pitched for under 11 – 20 yds/18.29 m
Pitched for under 9 – 18 yds/16.46 m
Height above playing surface – 27 in/68.58 cm

Each stump
Diameter – not less than 1¼ in/3.18 cm; nor more than 1⅜ in/3.49 cm

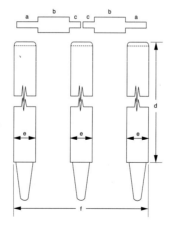

▲ *Fig. 2 Dimensions of stumps and bails*

Each bail
Overall length – 3¹³/₁₆ in/9.68 cm
Barrel length – 1¹³/₁₆ in/4.60 cm
Longer Spigot – 1¼ in/3.18 cm
Shorter Spigot – ¾ in/1.91 cm

5. Dispensing with bails
The umpires may agree to dispense with the use of bails, if necessary. If they so agree then no bails shall be used at either end. The use of bails shall be resumed as soon as conditions permit. *See* Law 28.4 (Dispensing with bails).

Bails

	Senior	Junior
Overall =	4⁵/₁₆ in/10.95 cm	3¹³/₁₆ in/9.68 cm
a =	1⅜ in/3.49 cm	1¼ in/3.18 cm
b =	2⅛ in/5.40 cm	1¹³/₁₆ in/4.60 cm
c =	1³/₁₆ in/2.06 cm	¾ in/1.91 cm

Stumps

	Senior	Junior
Height (d) =	28 in/71.1 cm	27 in/68.58 cm
Diameter (e) =		
max.	1½ in/3.81 cm	1⅜ in/3.49 cm
min.	1⅜ in/3.49 cm	1¼ in/3.18 cm
Overall width (f) of wicket	9 in/22.86 cm	8 in/20.32 cm

Law 9 – the bowling, popping and return creases

1. The creases

A bowling crease, a popping crease and two return creases shall be marked in white, as set out in **2**, **3** and **4** below, at each end of the pitch. *See* fig. 3.

2. The bowling crease

The bowling crease, which is the back edge of the crease marking, shall be the line through the centres of the three stumps at that end. It shall be 8ft 8 in/2.64 m in length, with the stumps in the centre.

3. The popping crease

The popping crease, which is the back edge of the crease marking, shall be in front of and parallel to the bowling crease and shall be 4 ft/1.22 m from it. The popping crease shall be marked to a minimum of 6 ft/1.83 m on either side of the imaginary line joining the centres of the middle stumps and shall be considered to be unlimited in length.

4. The return creases

The return creases, which are the inside edges of the crease markings, shall be at right angles to the popping crease at a distance of 4ft 4in/1.32m either side of the imaginary line joining the centres of the two middle stumps. Each return crease shall be marked from the popping crease to a minimum of 8 ft/2.44 m behind it and shall be considered to be unlimited in length.

▶ *Fig. 3 Dimensions of pitch, wicket and creases*

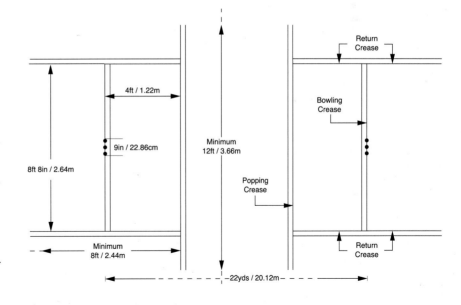

Law 10 – preparation and maintenance of the playing area

1. Rolling

The pitch shall not be rolled during the match except as permitted in **a** and **b** below.

a *Frequency and duration of rolling*: During the match the pitch may be rolled at the request of the captain of the batting side, for a period of not more than 7 minutes, before the start of each innings, other than the first innings of the match, and before the start of each subsequent day's play. *See* **d** below.

b *Rolling after a delayed start*: In addition to the rolling permitted above, if, after the toss and before the first innings of the match, the start is delayed, the captain of the batting side may request to have the pitch rolled for not more than 7 minutes. However, if the umpires together agree that the delay has had no significant effect on the state of the pitch, they shall refuse the request for the rolling of the pitch.

c *Choice of rollers*: If there is more than one roller available the captain of the batting side shall have the choice.

d *Timing of permitted rolling*: The rolling permitted (maximum 7 minutes) before play begins on any day shall be started not more than 30 minutes before the time scheduled or rescheduled for play to begin. The captain of the batting side may, however, delay the start of such rolling until not less than 10 minutes before the time scheduled or rescheduled for play to begin, should he so desire.

e *Insufficient time to complete rolling*: If a captain declares an innings closed, or forfeits an innings, or enforces the follow-on, and the other captain is prevented thereby from exercising his option of the rolling permitted (maximum 7 minutes), or if he is so prevented for any other reason, the extra time required to complete the rolling shall be taken out of the normal playing time.

2. Sweeping

a If rolling is to take place the pitch shall first be swept to avoid any possible damage by rolling in debris. This sweeping shall be done so that the 7 minutes allowed for rolling is not affected.

b The pitch shall be cleared of any debris at all intervals for meals, between innings and at the beginning of each day, not earlier than 30 minutes nor later than 10 minutes before the time scheduled or rescheduled for play to begin. *See* Law 15.1 (An interval).

c Notwithstanding the provisions of **a** and **b** above, the umpires shall not allow sweeping to take place where they consider it may be detrimental to the surface of the pitch.

3. Mowing

a *The pitch*: The pitch shall be mown on each day of the match on which play is expected to take place, if ground and weather conditions allow.

b *The outfield*: In order to ensure that conditions are as similar as possible for both sides, the outfield shall be mown on each day of the match on which play is expected to take place, if ground and weather conditions allow.

If, for reasons other than ground and weather conditions, complete mowing of the outfield is not possible, the Ground Authority shall notify the captains and umpires of the procedure to be adopted for such mowing during the match.

c *Responsibility for mowing*: All mowings which are carried out before the match shall be the responsibility of the Ground Authority. All subsequent mowings shall be carried out under the supervision of the umpires.

d *Timing of mowing:*
(i) Mowing of the pitch on any day of the match shall be completed not later than 30 minutes before the time scheduled or rescheduled for play to begin on that day.
(ii) Mowing of the outfield on any day of the match shall be completed not later than 15 minutes before the time scheduled or rescheduled for play to begin on that day.

4. Watering
The pitch shall not be watered during the match.

5. Re-marking creases
The creases shall be re-marked whenever either umpire considers it necessary.

6. Maintenance of footholes
The umpires shall ensure that the holes made by the bowlers and batsmen are cleaned out and dried whenever necessary to facilitate play. In matches of more than one day's duration, the umpires shall allow, if necessary, the re-turfing of footholes made by the bowler in his delivery stride, or the use of quick-setting fillings for the same purpose.

7. Securing of footholds and maintenance of pitch
During play, the umpires shall allow the players to secure their footholds by the use of sawdust provided that no damage to the pitch is caused and that Law 42 (Fair and unfair play) is not contravened.

8. Non-turf pitches
Wherever appropriate, the provisions set out in **1** to **7** above shall apply.

Law 11 –
covering the pitch

1. Before the match
The use of covers before the match is the responsibility of the Ground Authority and may include full covering if required. However, the Ground Authority shall grant suitable facility to the captains to inspect the pitch before the nomination of their players and to the umpires to discharge their duties as laid down in Laws 3 (The umpires), 7 (The pitch), **8** (The wickets), 9 (The bowling, popping and return creases) and 10 (Preparation and maintenance of the playing area).

2. During the match
The pitch shall not be completely covered during the match unless provided otherwise by regulations or by agreement before the toss.

3. Covering bowlers' run ups
Whenever possible, the bowlers' run ups shall be covered in inclement weather, in order to keep them dry. Unless there is agreement for full covering under **2** above the covers so used shall not extend further than 5 ft/1.52 m in front of each popping crease.

4. Removal of covers
a If after the toss the pitch is covered overnight, the covers shall be removed in the morning at the earliest possible moment on each day that play is expected to take place.
b If covers are used during the day as protection from inclement weather, or if inclement weather delays the removal of overnight covers, they shall be removed promptly as soon as conditions allow.

Law 12 – innings

1. Number of innings
a A match shall be one or two innings of each side according to agreement reached before the match.
b It may be agreed to limit any innings to a number of overs or by a period of time. If such an agreement is made then:
(i) in a one innings match it shall apply to both innings
(ii) in a two innings match it shall apply to either the first innings of each side; or the second innings of each side; or both innings of each side.

2. Alternate innings
In a two innings match each side shall take their innings alternately except in the cases provided for in Law 13 (The follow-on) or Law 14.2 (Forfeiture of an innings).

3. Completed innings
A side's innings is to be considered as completed if:
a the side is all out; or
b at the fall of a wicket, further balls remain to be bowled, but no further batsman is available to come in; or
c the captain declares the innings closed; or
d the captain forfeits the innings; or

e in the case of an agreement under **1b** above, either (i) the prescribed number of overs has been bowled or (ii) the prescribed time has expired.

4. The toss
The captains shall toss for the choice of innings on the field of play not earlier than 30 minutes, nor later than 15 minutes, before the scheduled or any rescheduled time for the match to start. Note, however, the provisions of Law 1.3 (Captain).

5. Decision to be notified
The captain of the side winning the toss shall notify the opposing captain of his decision to bat or to field, not later than 10 minutes before the scheduled or any rescheduled time for the match to start. Once notified the decision may not be altered.

Law 13 – the follow-on

1. Lead on first innings
a In a two innings match of 5 days or more, the side which bats first and leads by at least 200 runs shall have the option of requiring the other side to follow their innings.
b The same option shall be available in two

innings matches of shorter duration with the minimum required leads as follows:
(i) 150 runs in a match of 3 or 4 days
(ii) 100 runs in a 2-day match
(iii) 75 runs in a 1-day match.

2. Notification
A captain shall notify the opposing captain and the umpires of his intention to take up this option. Law 10.1**e** (Insufficient time to complete rolling) shall apply.

3. First day's play lost
If no play takes place on the first day of a match of more than one day's duration, **1** above shall apply in accordance with the number of days remaining from the actual start of the match. The day on which play first commences shall count as a whole day for this purpose, irrespective of the time at which play starts.

Play will have taken place as soon as, after the call of Play, the first over has started. *See* Law 22.2 (Start of an over).

Law 14 – declaration and forfeiture

1. Time of declaration
The captain of the batting side may declare an innings closed, when the ball is dead, at any time during a match.

2. Forfeiture of an innings
A captain may forfeit either of his side's innings. A forfeited innings shall be considered as a completed innings.

3. Notification
A captain shall notify the opposing captain and the umpires of his decision to declare or to forfeit an innings. Law 10.1e (Insufficient time to complete rolling) shall apply.

Law 15 – intervals

1. An interval
The following shall be classed as intervals:
(i) the period between close of play on one day and the start of the next day's play
(ii) intervals between innings
(iii) intervals for meals
(iv) intervals for drinks
(v) any other agreed interval.

All these intervals shall be considered as scheduled breaks for the purposes of Law 2.5 (Fielder absent or leaving the field).

2. Agreement of intervals
a Before the toss:
(i) the hours of play shall be established
(ii) except as in **b** below, the timing and duration of intervals for meals shall be agreed
(iii) the timing and duration of any other interval under 1(v) above shall be agreed.
b In a one-day match no specific time need be agreed for the tea interval. It may be agreed instead to take this interval between the innings.
c Intervals for drinks may not be taken during the last hour of the match, as defined in Law 16.6 (Last hour of match – number of overs). Subject to this limitation the captains and umpires shall agree the times for such intervals, if any, before the toss and on each subsequent day not later than 10 minutes before play is scheduled to start. *See* also Law 3.3 (Agreement with captains).

3. Duration of intervals
a An interval for lunch or for tea shall be of the duration agreed under 2**a** above, taken from the call of Time before the interval until the call of Play on resumption after the interval.
b An interval between innings shall be 10 minutes from the close of an innings to the call of Play for the start of the next innings, except as in **4**, **6** and **7** below.

4. No allowance for interval between innings
In addition to the provisions of **6** and **7** below,
a if an innings ends when 10 minutes or less remain before the time agreed for close of play on any day, there will be no further play on that day. No change will be made to the time for the start of play on the following day on account of the 10 minutes between innings
b if a captain declares an innings closed during an interruption in play of more than 10 minutes duration, no adjustment shall be made to the time for resumption of play on account of the 10 minutes between innings, which shall be considered as included in the interruption. Law 10.1**e** (Insufficient time to complete rolling) shall apply
c if a captain declares an innings closed during any interval other than an interval for drinks, the interval shall be of the agreed duration and shall be considered to include the 10 minutes between innings.

Law 10.1e (Insufficient time to complete rolling) shall apply.

5. Changing agreed times for intervals

If for adverse conditions of ground, weather or light, or for any other reason, playing time is lost, the umpires and captains together may alter the time of the lunch interval or of the tea interval. See also **6**, **7** and **9c** below.

6. Changing agreed time for lunch interval

a If an innings ends when 10 minutes or less remain before the agreed time for lunch, the interval shall be taken immediately. It shall be of the agreed length and shall be considered to include the 10 minutes between innings.

b If, because of adverse conditions of ground, weather or light, or in exceptional circumstances, a stoppage occurs when 10 minutes or less remain before the agreed time for lunch then, notwithstanding **5** above, the interval shall be taken immediately. It shall be of the agreed length. Play shall resume at the end of this interval or as soon after as conditions permit.

c If the players have occasion to leave the field for any reason when more than 10 minutes remain before the agreed time for lunch then, unless the umpires and captains together agree to alter it, lunch will be taken at the agreed time.

7. Changing agreed time for tea interval

a (i) If an innings ends when 30 minutes or less remain before the agreed time for tea, then the interval shall be taken immediately. It shall be of the agreed length and shall be considered to include the 10 minutes between innings.

(ii) If, when 30 minutes remain before the agreed time for tea, an interval between innings is already in progress, play will resume at the end of the 10 minute interval.

b (i) If, because of adverse conditions of ground, weather or light, or in exceptional circumstances, a stoppage occurs when 30 minutes or less remain before the agreed time for tea, then unless either there is an agreement to change the time for tea, as permitted in 5 above, or the captains agree to forgo the tea interval, as permitted in **10** below, the interval shall be taken immediately. The interval shall be of the agreed length. Play shall resume at the end of this interval or as soon after as conditions permit.

(ii) If a stoppage is already in progress when 30 minutes remain before the time agreed for tea, **5** above will apply.

8. Tea interval – 9 wickets down

If *either*: 9 wickets are already down when 2 minutes remain to the agreed time; *or*: the 9th wicket falls within these 2 minutes or at any later time up to and including the final ball of the over in progress at the agreed time for tea;

then notwithstanding the provisions of Law 16.5(b) (Completion of an over), tea will not be taken until the end of the over in progress 30 minutes after the originally agreed time for tea, unless the players have cause to leave the field of play, or the innings is concluded earlier.

9. Intervals for drinks

a If on any day the captains agree that there shall be intervals for drinks, the option to take such intervals shall be available to either side. Each interval shall be kept as short as possible and in any case shall not exceed 5 minutes.

b (i) Unless both captains agree to forgo any drinks interval, it shall be taken at the end of the over in progress when the agreed time is reached. If, however, a wicket falls within 5 minutes of the agreed time then drinks shall be taken immediately. No other variation in the timing of drinks intervals shall be permitted except as provided for in **c** below.

(ii) For the purpose of (i) above and Law 3.9**a**(ii) (Suspension of play for adverse conditions of ground, weather or light) only, the batsmen at the wicket may deputise for their captain.

c If an innings ends or the players have to leave the field of play for any other reason within 30 minutes of the agreed time for a drinks interval, the umpires and captains together may rearrange the timing of drinks intervals in that session.

10. Agreement to forgo intervals

At any time during the match, the captains may agree to forgo the tea interval or any of the drinks intervals. The umpires shall be informed of the decision.

11. Scorers to be informed

The umpires shall ensure that the scorers are informed of all agreements about hours of play and intervals, and of any changes made thereto as permitted under this Law.

Law 16 – start of play; cessation of play

1. Call of Play

The umpire at the bowler's end shall call Play at the start of the match and on the resumption of play after any interval or interruption.

2. Call of Time

The umpire at the bowler's end shall call Time on the cessation of play before any interval or interruption of play and at the conclusion of the match. *See* Law 27 (Appeals).

3. Removal of bails

After the call of Time, the bails shall be removed from both wickets.

4. Starting a new over

Another over shall always be started at any time during the match, unless an interval is to be taken in the circumstances set out in **5** below, if the umpire, after walking at his normal pace, has arrived at his position behind the stumps at the bowler's end before the time agreed for the next interval, or for the close of play, has been reached.

5. Completion of an over

Other than at the end of the match,

a if the agreed time for an interval is reached during an over, the over shall be completed before the interval is taken except as provided for in **b** below

b when less than 2 minutes remain before the time agreed for the next interval, the interval will be taken immediately if, either

(i) a batsman is out or retires, or

(ii) the players have occasion to leave the field

whether this occurs during an over or at the end of an over. Except at the end of an innings, if an over is thus interrupted it shall be completed on resumption of play.

6. Last hour of match – number of overs

When one hour of playing time of the match remains, according to the agreed hours of play, the over in progress shall be completed. The next over shall be the first of a minimum of 20 overs which must be bowled, provided that a result is not reached earlier and provided that there is no interval or interruption in play.

The umpire at the bowler's end shall indicate the commencement of this 20 overs to the players and the scorers. The period of play thereafter shall be referred to as the last hour, whatever its actual duration.

7. Last hour of match – interruptions of play

If there is an interruption in play during the last hour of the match, the minimum number of overs to be bowled shall be reduced from 20 as follows.

a The time lost for an interruption is counted from the call of Time until the time for resumption of play as decided by the umpires.
b One over shall be deducted for every complete 3 minutes of time lost.
c In the case of more than one such interruption, the minutes lost shall not be aggregated; the calculation shall be made for each interruption separately.
d If, when one hour of playing time remains, an interruption is already in progress,
(i) only the time lost after this moment shall be counted in the calculation
(ii) the over in progress at the start of the interruption shall be completed on resumption of play and shall not count as one of the minimum number of overs to be bowled.
e If, after the start of the last hour, an interruption occurs during an over, the over shall be completed on resumption of play. The two part-overs shall between them count as one over of the minimum number to be bowled.

8. Last hour of match – intervals between innings

If an innings ends so that a new innings is to be started during the last hour of the match, the interval starts with the end of the innings and is to end 10 minutes later.
a If this interval is already in progress at the start of the last hour, then to determine the number of overs to be bowled in the new innings, calculations are to be made as set out in **7** above.
b If the innings ends after the last hour has started, two calculations are to be made, as set out in **c** and **d** below. The greater of the numbers yielded by these two calculations is to be the minimum number of overs to be bowled in the new innings.
c Calculation based on overs remaining:
(i) at the conclusion of the innings, the number of overs that remain to be bowled, of the minimum in the last hour, to be noted
(ii) if this is not a whole number it is to be rounded up to the next whole number
(iii) three overs to be deducted from the result for the interval.
d Calculation based on time remaining:
(i) at the conclusion of the innings, the time remaining until the agreed time for close of play to be noted
(ii) ten minutes to be deducted from this time, for the interval, to determine the playing time remaining
(iii) a calculation to be made of one over for every complete 3 minutes of the playing time remaining, plus one more over for any further part of 3 minutes remaining.

9. Conclusion of match
The match is concluded:

a as soon as a result, as defined in sections **1, 2, 3** or **4** of Law 21 (The result), is reached.
b as soon as both:
(i) the minimum number of overs for the last hour are completed, and
(ii) the agreed time for close of play is reached –
unless a result has been reached earlier
c if, without the match being concluded either as in **a** or in **b** above, the players leave the field, either for adverse conditions of ground, weather or light, or in exceptional circumstances, and no further play is possible thereafter.

10. Completion of last over of match
The over in progress at the close of play on the final day shall be completed unless either (i) a result has been reached, or
(ii) the players have occasion to leave the field. In this case there shall be no resumption of play, except in the circumstances of Law 21.9 (Mistakes in scoring), and the match shall be at an end.

11. Bowler unable to complete an over during last hour of match
If, for any reason, a bowler is unable to complete an over during the last hour, Law 22.8 (Bowler incapacitated or suspended during an over) shall apply.

Law 17 – practice on the field

1. Practice on the field

a There shall be no bowling or batting practice on the pitch, or on the area parallel and immediately adjacent to the pitch, at any time on any day of the match.

b There shall be no bowling or batting practice on any other part of the square on any day of the match, except before the start of play or after the close of play on that day. Practice before the start of play

(i) must not continue later than 30 minutes before the scheduled time or any rescheduled time for play to start on that day

(ii) shall not be allowed if the umpires consider that, in the prevailing conditions of ground and weather, it will be detrimental to the surface of the square.

c There shall be no practice on the field of play between the call of Play and the call of Time, if the umpire considers that it could result in a waste of time. *See* Law 42.9 (Time wasting by the fielding side).

d If a player contravenes **a** or **b** above he shall not be allowed to bowl until:

either: at least 1 hour later than the contravention;

or: there has been at least 30 minutes of playing time since the contravention; whichever is sooner. If an over is in progress at the contravention, he shall not be allowed to complete that over.

2. Trial run up

No bowler shall have a trial run up between the call of Play and the call of Time unless the umpire is satisfied that it will not cause any waste of time.

Law 18 – scoring runs

1. A run

The score shall be reckoned by runs. A run is scored:

a so often as the batsmen, at any time while the ball is in play, have crossed and made good their ground from end to end

b when a boundary is scored. *See* Law 19 (Boundaries)

c when penalty runs are awarded. *See* **6** below

d when Lost ball is called. *See* Law 20 (Lost ball).

2. Runs disallowed

Notwithstanding **1** above, or any other provisions elsewhere in the Laws, the scoring of runs or awarding of penalties will be subject to any disallowance of runs provided for within the Laws that may be applicable.

3. Short runs

a A run is short if a batsman fails to make good his ground on turning for a further run.

b Although a short run shortens the succeeding one, the latter if completed shall not be regarded as short. A striker taking stance in front of his popping crease may run from that point also without penalty.

4. Unintentional short runs

Except in the circumstances of **5** below,

a if either batsman runs a short run, unless a boundary is scored the umpire concerned shall call and signal Short run as soon as the ball becomes dead and that run shall not be scored

b if, after either or both batsmen run short, a boundary is scored, the umpire concerned shall disregard the short running and shall not call or signal Short run

c if both batsmen run short in one and the same run, this shall be regarded as only one short run

d if more than one run is short then, subject to **b** and **c** above, all runs so called shall not be scored.

If there has been more than one short run the umpire shall inform the scorers as to the number of runs scored.

5. Deliberate short runs

a Notwithstanding **4** above, if either umpire considers that either or both batsmen deliberately run short at his end, the following procedure shall be adopted.

(i) The umpire concerned shall, when the ball is dead, warn the batsmen that the practice is unfair, indicate that this is a first and final warning and inform the other umpire of what has occurred. This warning shall continue to apply throughout the innings. The umpire shall so inform each incoming batsman.

(ii) The batsmen shall return to their original ends.

(iii) Whether a batsman is dismissed or not, the umpire at the bowler's end shall disallow all runs to the batting side from that delivery other than the penalty for a No ball or Wide, or penalties under Laws 42.5 (Deliberate distraction or obstruction of batsman) and 42.13 (Fielders damaging the pitch), if applicable.

(iv) The umpire at the bowler's end shall inform the scorers as to the number of runs scored.

b If there is any further instance of deliberate short running by any batsman in that innings, when the ball is dead the umpire concerned shall inform the other umpire of what has occurred and the procedure set out in **a**(ii) and (iii) above shall be repeated. Additionally, the umpire at the bowler's end shall:

(i) award 5 penalty runs to the fielding side. *See* Law 42.17 (Penalty runs)

(ii) inform the scorers as to the number of runs scored

(iii) inform the batsmen, the captain of the fielding side and, as soon as practicable, the captain of the batting side of the reason for this action

(iv) report the occurrence, with the other umpire, to the Executive of the batting side and any Governing Body responsible for the match, who shall take such action as is considered appropriate against the captain and player or players concerned.

6. Runs scored for penalties

Runs shall be scored for penalties under **5** above and Laws 2.6 (Player returning without permission), 24 (No ball), 25 (Wide ball), 41.2 (Fielding the ball), 41.3 (Protective helmets belonging to the fielding side) and 42 (Fair and unfair play).

7. Runs scored for boundaries

Runs shall be scored for boundary allowances under Law 19 (Boundaries).

8. Runs scored for Lost ball

Runs shall be scored when Lost ball is called under Law 20 (Lost ball).

9. Batsman dismissed

When either batsman is dismissed:

a any penalties to either side that may be applicable shall stand but no other runs shall be scored, except as stated in **10** below. Note, however, Law 42.17b (Penalty runs)

b 12a below will apply if the method of dismissal is Caught, Handled the ball or Obstructing the field. 12a will also apply if a batsman is Run out, except in the circumstances of Law 2.8 (Transgression of the Laws by a batsman who has a runner) where 12b below will apply

c the not out batsman shall return to his original end except as stated in **b** above.

10. Runs scored when a batsman is dismissed

In addition to any penalties to either side that may be applicable, if a batsman is:

a dismissed Handled the ball, the batting side shall score the runs completed before the offence

b dismissed Obstructing the field, the bat-

ting side shall score the runs completed before the offence. If, however, the obstruction prevents a catch from being made, no runs other than penalties shall be scored
c dismissed Run out, the batting side shall score the runs completed before the dismissal. If, however, a striker with a runner is himself dismissed Run out, no runs other than penalties shall be scored. *See* Law 2.8 (Transgression of the Laws by a batsman who has a runner).

11. Runs scored when ball becomes dead
a When the ball becomes dead on the fall of a wicket, runs shall be scored as laid down in **9** and **10** above.
b When the ball becomes dead for any reason other than the fall of a wicket, or is called dead by an umpire, unless there is specific provision otherwise in the Laws, the batting side shall be credited with
(i) all runs completed by the batsmen before the incident or call, and
(ii) the run in progress if the batsmen have crossed at the instant of the incident or call. Note specifically, however, the provisions of Laws 34.4c (Runs permitted from ball lawfully struck more than once) and 42.5b (iii) (Deliberate distraction or obstruction of batsman), and
(iii) any penalties that are applicable.

12. Batsman returning to wicket he has left
a If, while the ball is in play, the batsmen have crossed in running, neither shall return to the wicket he has left, except as in **b** below.
b The batsmen shall return to the wickets they originally left in the cases of, and only in the cases of:
(i) a boundary
(ii) disallowance of runs for any reason
(iii) the dismissal of a batsman, except as in 9**b** above.

Law 19 – boundaries

1. The boundary of the field of play
a Before the toss, the umpires shall agree the boundary of the field of play with both captains. The boundary shall if possible be marked along its whole length.
b The boundary shall be agreed so that no part of any sight-screen is within the field of play.
c An obstacle or person within the field of play shall not be regarded as a boundary unless so decided by the umpires before the toss. *See* Law 3.4(ii) (To inform captains and scorers).

2. Defining the boundary – boundary marking
a Wherever practicable the boundary shall be marked by means of a white line or a rope laid along the ground.
b If the boundary is marked by a white line,
(i) the inside edge of the line shall be the boundary edge
(ii) a flag, post or board used merely to highlight the position of a line marked on the ground must be placed outside the boundary edge and is not itself to be regarded as defining or marking the boundary. Note, however, the provisions of **c** below.
c If a solid object is used to mark the boundary, it must have an edge or a line to constitute the boundary edge
(i) for a rope, which includes any similar object of curved cross section lying on the ground, the boundary edge will be the line formed by the innermost points of the rope along its length
(ii) for a fence, which includes any similar object in contact with the ground, but with a flat surface projecting above the ground, the boundary edge will be the base line of the fence.
d If the boundary edge is not defined as in **b** or **c** above, the umpires and captains must agree, before the toss, what line will

be the boundary edge. Where there is no physical marker for a section of boundary, the boundary edge shall be the imaginary straight line joining the two nearest marked points of the boundary edge.

e If a solid object used to mark the boundary is disturbed for any reason during play, then if possible it shall be restored to its original position as soon as the ball is dead. If this is not possible, then

(i) if some part of the fence or other marker has come within the field of play, that portion is to be removed from the field of play as soon as the ball is dead

(ii) the line where the base of the fence or marker originally stood shall define the boundary edge.

3. Scoring a boundary

a A boundary shall be scored and signalled by the umpire at the bowler's end whenever, while the ball is in play, in his opinion:

(i) the ball touches the boundary, or is grounded beyond the boundary

(ii) a fielder, with some part of his person in contact with the ball, touches the boundary or has some part of his person grounded beyond the boundary.

b The phrases 'touches the boundary' and 'touching the boundary' shall mean contact with, either

(i) the boundary edge as defined in **2** above, or

(ii) any person or obstacle within the field of play which has been designated a boundary by the umpires before the toss.

c The phrase 'grounded beyond the boundary' shall mean contact with, either

(i) any part of a line or a solid object marking the boundary, except its boundary edge, or

(ii) the ground outside the boundary edge, or

(iii) any object in contact with the ground outside the boundary edge.

4. Runs allowed for boundaries

a Before the toss, the umpires shall agree with both captains the runs to be allowed for boundaries. In deciding the allowances, the umpires and captains shall be guided by the prevailing custom of the ground.

b Unless agreed differently under **a** above, the allowances for boundaries shall be 6 runs if the ball having been struck by the bat pitches beyond the boundary, but otherwise 4 runs. These allowances shall still apply even though the ball has previously touched a fielder. *See* also **c** below.

c The ball shall be regarded as pitching beyond the boundary and 6 runs shall be scored if a fielder:

(i) has any part of his person touching the boundary or grounded beyond the boundary when he catches the ball

(ii) catches the ball and subsequently touches the boundary or grounds some part of his person beyond the boundary while carrying the ball but before completing the catch. *See* Law 32 (Caught).

5. Runs scored

When a boundary is scored,

a the penalty for a No ball or a Wide, if applicable, shall stand together with any penalties under any of Laws 2.6 (Player returning without permission), 18.5b (Deliberate short runs) or 42 (Fair and unfair play) that apply before the boundary is scored

b the batting side, except in the circumstances of **6** below, shall additionally be awarded whichever is the greater of:

(i) the allowance for the boundary

(ii) the runs completed by the batsmen, together with the run in progress if they have crossed at the instant the boundary is scored. When these runs exceed the boundary allowance, they shall replace the boundary for the purposes of Law 18.12 (Batsman returning to wicket he has left).

6. Overthrow or wilful act of fielder

If the boundary results either from an overthrow or from the wilful act of a fielder the runs scored shall be:

(i) the penalty for a No ball or a Wide, if applicable, and penalties under any of Laws 2.6 (Player returning without permission), 18.5**b** (Deliberate short runs) or 42 (Fair and unfair play) that are applicable before the boundary is scored, and
(ii) the allowance for the boundary, and
(iii) the runs completed by the batsmen, together with the run in progress if they have crossed at the instant of the throw or act.

Law 18.12**a** (Batsman returning to wicket he has left) shall apply as from the instant of the throw or act.

Law 20 – lost ball

1. Fielder to call Lost ball

If a ball in play cannot be found or recovered, any fielder may call Lost ball. The ball shall then become dead. *See* Law 23.1 (Ball is dead). Law 18.12**a** (Batsman returning to wicket he has left) shall apply as from the instant of the call.

2. Ball to be replaced

The umpires shall replace the ball with one which has had wear comparable with that which the previous ball had received before it was lost or became irrecoverable. *See* Law 5.5 (Ball lost or becoming unfit for play).

3. Runs scored

a The penalty for a No ball or a Wide, if applicable, shall stand, together with any penalties under any of Laws 2.6 (Player returning without permission), 18.5**b** (Deliberate short runs) or 42 (Fair and unfair play) that are applicable before the call of Lost ball.
b The batting side shall additionally be awarded, either
(i) the runs completed by the batsmen, together with the run in progress if they have crossed at the instant of the call, or
(ii) 6 runs,
whichever is the greater.

4. How scored

If there is a one run penalty for a No ball or for a Wide, it shall be scored as a No ball extra or as a Wide as appropriate. *See* Laws 24.13 (Runs resulting from a No ball – how scored) and 25.6 (Runs resulting from a Wide – how scored). If any other penalties have been awarded to either side, they shall be scored as penalty extras. *See* Law 42.17 (Penalty runs).

Runs to the batting side in 3**b** above shall be credited to the striker if the ball has been struck by the bat, but otherwise to the total of Byes, Leg byes, No balls or Wides as the case may be.

Law 21 – the result

1. A Win – two innings match

The side which has scored a total of runs in excess of that scored in the two completed innings of the opposing side shall win the match. Note also **6** below.

A forfeited innings is to count as a completed innings. *See* Law 14 (Declaration and forfeiture).

2. A Win – one innings match

The side which has scored in its one innings a total of runs in excess of that scored by the opposing side in its one completed innings shall win the match. Note also **6** below.

3. Umpires awarding a match

a A match shall be lost by a side which, either
(i) concedes defeat, or
(ii) in the opinion of the umpires refuses to play,
and the umpires shall award the match to the other side.

b If an umpire considers that an action by any player or players might constitute a refusal by either side to play then the umpires together shall ascertain the cause of the action. If they then decide together that this action does constitute a refusal to play by one side, they shall so inform the captain of that side. If the captain persists in the action the umpires shall award the match in accordance with **a**(ii) above.

c If action as in **b** above takes place after play has started and does not constitute a refusal to play:

(i) playing time lost shall be counted from the start of the action until play recommences, subject to Law 15.5 (Changing agreed times for intervals)

(ii) the time for close of play on that day shall be extended by this length of time, subject to Law 3.9 (Suspension of play for adverse conditions of ground, weather or light)

(iii) if applicable, no overs shall be deducted during the last hour of the match solely on account of this time.

4. A Tie

The result of a match shall be a Tie when the scores are equal at the conclusion of play, but only if the side batting last has completed its innings.

5. A Draw

A match which is concluded, as defined in Law 16.9 (Conclusion of a match), without being determined in any of the ways stated in **1**, **2**, **3** or **4** above, shall count as a Draw.

6. Winning hit or extras

a As soon as a result is reached, as defined in **1**, **2**, **3** or **4** above, the match is at an end. Nothing that happens thereafter, except as in Law 42.17(b), shall be regarded as part of it. Note also **9** below.

b The side batting last will have scored enough runs to win only if its total of runs is sufficient without including any runs completed before the dismissal of the striker by the completion of a catch or by the obstruction of a catch.

c If a boundary is scored before the batsmen have completed sufficient runs to win the match, then the whole of the boundary allowance shall be credited to the side's total and, in the case of a hit by the bat, to the striker's score.

7. Statement of result

If the side batting last wins the match without losing all its wickets, the result shall be stated as a win by the number of wickets still then to fall.

If the side batting last has lost all its wickets, but, as the result of an award of 5 penalty runs at the end of the match, has scored a total of runs in excess of the total scored by the opposing side, the result shall be stated as a win to that side by Penalty runs.

If the side fielding last wins the match, the result shall be stated as a win by runs.

If the match is decided by one side conceding defeat or refusing to play, the result shall be stated as Match Conceded or Match Awarded as the case may be.

8. Correctness of result

Any decision as to the correctness of the scores shall be the responsibility of the umpires. *See* Law 3.15 (Correctness of scores).

9. Mistakes in scoring

If, after the umpires and players have left the field in the belief that the match has been concluded, the umpires discover that a mistake in scoring has occurred which affects the result, then, subject to **10** below, they shall adopt the following procedure.

a If, when the players leave the field, the side batting last has not completed its innings, and either

(i) the number of overs to be bowled in the last hour has not been completed, or

(ii) the agreed finishing time has not been reached,

then unless one side concedes defeat the umpires shall order play to resume.

If conditions permit, play will then continue until the prescribed number of overs has been completed and the time remaining has elapsed, unless a result is reached earlier. The number of overs and/or the time remaining shall be taken as they were when the players left the field; no account shall be taken of the time between that moment and the resumption of play.

b If, when the players leave the field, the overs have been completed and time has been reached, or if the side batting last has completed its innings, the umpires shall immediately inform both captains of the necessary corrections to the scores and to the result.

10. Result not to be changed

Once the umpires have agreed with the scorers the correctness of the scores at the conclusion of the match – *see* Laws 3.15 (Correctness of scores) and 4.2 (Correctness of scores) – the result cannot thereafter be changed.

Law 22 – the over

1. Number of balls

The ball shall be bowled from each wicket alternately in overs of 6 balls.

2. Start of an over

An over has started when the bowler starts his run up or, if he has no run up, his delivery action for the first delivery of that over.

3. Call of Over

When 6 balls have been bowled other than those which are not to count in the over and as the ball becomes dead – *see* Law 23 (Dead ball) – the umpire shall call Over before leaving the wicket.

4. Balls not to count in the over

a A ball shall not count as one of the 6 balls of the over unless it is delivered, even though a batsman may be dismissed or some other incident occurs before the ball is delivered.

b A ball which is delivered by the bowler shall not count as one of the 6 balls of the over

(i) if it is called dead, or is to be considered dead, before the striker has had an opportunity to play it. *See* Law 23 (Dead ball)

(ii) if it is a No ball. *See* Law 24 (No ball)

(iii) if it is a Wide. *See* Law 25 (Wide ball)

(iv) if it is called dead in the circumstances of Law 23.3(b)(vi) (Umpire calling and signalling Dead ball)

(v) when 5 penalty runs are awarded to the batting side under any of Laws 2.6 (Player returning without permission), 41.2 (Fielding the ball), 42.4 (Deliberate distraction or obstruction of batsman).

5. Umpire miscounting

If an umpire miscounts the number of balls, the over as counted by the umpire shall stand.

6. Bowler changing ends

A bowler shall be allowed to change ends as often as desired, provided only that he does not bowl two overs, or parts thereof, consecutively in the same innings.

7. Finishing an over

a Other than at the end of an innings, a bowler shall finish an over in progress unless he is incapacitated, or he is suspended under any of Laws 17.1 (Practice on the field), 42.7 (Dangerous and unfair bowling – action by the umpire), 42.9 (Time wasting by the fielding side), or 42.12 (Bowler running on the protected area after delivering the ball).

b If for any reason, other than the end of an

innings, an over is left uncompleted at the start of an interval or interruption of play, it shall be completed on resumption of play.

8. Bowler incapacitated or suspended during an over

If for any reason a bowler is incapacitated while running up to bowl the first ball of an over, or is incapacitated or suspended during an over, the umpire shall call and signal Dead ball. Another bowler shall complete the over from the same end, provided that he does not bowl two overs, or parts thereof, consecutively in one innings.

Law 23 – dead ball

1. Ball is dead
a The ball becomes dead when:
(i) it is finally settled in the hands of the wicket-keeper or the bowler
(ii) a boundary is scored. *See* Law 19.3 (Scoring a boundary)
(iii) a batsman is dismissed
(iv) whether played or not it becomes trapped between the bat and person of a batsman or between items of his clothing or equipment
(v) whether played or not it lodges in the clothing or equipment of a batsman or the clothing of an umpire

(vi) it lodges in a protective helmet worn by a member of the fielding side
(vii) there is a contravention of either of Laws 41.2 (Fielding the ball) or 41.3 (Protective helmets belonging to the fielding side)
(viii) there is an award of penalty runs under Law 2.6 (Player returning without permission)
(ix) Lost ball is called. *See* Law 20 (Lost ball)
(x) the umpire calls Over or Time.
b The ball shall be considered to be dead when it is clear to the umpire at the bowler's end that the fielding side and both batsmen at the wicket have ceased to regard it as in play.

2. Ball finally settled
Whether the ball is finally settled or not is a matter for the umpire alone to decide.

3. Umpire calling and signalling Dead ball
a When the ball has become dead under **1** above, the bowler's end umpire may call Dead ball, if it is necessary to inform the players.
b Either umpire shall call and signal Dead ball when:
(i) he intervenes in a case of unfair play
(ii) a serious injury to a player or umpire occurs

(iii) he leaves his normal position for consultation
(iv) one or both bails fall from the striker's wicket before he has the opportunity of playing the ball
(v) he is satisfied that for an adequate reason the striker is not ready for the delivery of the ball and, if the ball is delivered, makes no attempt to play it
(vi) the striker is distracted by any noise or movement or in any other way while he is preparing to receive or receiving a delivery. This shall apply whether the source of the distraction is within the game or outside it. Note, however, the provisions of Law 42.4 (Deliberate attempt to distract the striker).
The ball shall not count as one of the over
(vii) the bowler drops the ball accidentally before delivery
(viii) the ball does not leave the bowler's hand for any reason other than an attempt to run out the non-striker before entering his delivery stride. *See* Law 42.15 (Bowler attempting to run out non-striker before delivery)
(ix) he is required to do so under any of the Laws.

4. Ball ceases to be dead
The ball ceases to be dead – that is, it comes into play – when the bowler starts his run up or, if he has no run up, his bowling action.

5. Action on call of Dead ball

a A ball is not to count as one of the over if it becomes dead or is to be considered dead before the striker has had an opportunity to play it.

b If the ball becomes dead or is to be considered dead after the striker has had an opportunity to play the ball, except in the circumstances of 3(vi) above and Law 42.4 (Deliberate attempt to distract striker), no additional delivery shall be allowed unless No ball or Wide has been called.

Law 24 – no ball

1. Mode of delivery

a The umpire shall ascertain whether the bowler intends to bowl right handed or left handed, over or round the wicket, and shall so inform the striker.

It is unfair if the bowler fails to notify the umpire of a change in his mode of delivery. In this case the umpire shall call and signal No ball.

b Underarm bowling shall not be permitted except by special agreement before the match.

2. Fair delivery – the arm

For a delivery to be fair in respect of the arm the ball must not be thrown. *See* **3** below.

Although it is the primary responsibility of the striker's end umpire to ensure the fairness of a delivery in this respect, there is nothing in this Law to debar the bowler's end umpire from calling and signalling No ball if he considers that the ball has been thrown.

a If, in the opinion of either umpire, the ball has been thrown, he shall

(i) call and signal No ball

(ii) caution the bowler, when the ball is dead. This caution shall apply throughout the innings

(iii) inform the other umpire, the batsmen at the wicket, the captain of the fielding side and, as soon as practicable, the captain of the batting side of what has occurred.

b If either umpire considers that after such caution a further delivery by the same bowler in that innings is thrown, the umpire concerned shall repeat the procedure set out in **a** above, indicating to the bowler that this is a final warning. This warning shall also apply throughout the innings.

c If either umpire considers that a further delivery by the same bowler in that innings is thrown,

(i) the umpire concerned shall call and signal No ball. When the ball is dead he shall

inform the other umpire, the batsmen at the wicket and, as soon as practicable, the captain of the batting side of what has occurred

(ii) the umpire at the bowler's end shall direct the captain of the fielding side to take the bowler off forthwith. The over shall be completed by another bowler, who shall neither have bowled the previous over nor be allowed to bowl the next over. The bowler thus taken off shall not bowl again in that innings

(iii) the umpires together shall report the occurrence as soon as possible to the Executive of the fielding side and any Governing Body responsible for the match, who shall take such action as is considered appropriate against the captain and bowler concerned.

3. Definition of fair delivery – the arm

A ball is fairly delivered in respect of the arm if, once the bowler's arm has reached the level of the shoulder in the delivery swing, the elbow joint is not straightened partially or completely from that point until the ball has left the hand. This definition shall not debar a bowler from flexing or rotating the wrist in the delivery swing.

4. Bowler throwing towards striker's end before delivery

If the bowler throws the ball towards the striker's end before entering his delivery stride, either umpire shall call and signal No ball. *See* Law 42.16 (Batsmen stealing a run). However, the procedure stated in **2** above of caution, informing, final warning, action against the bowler and reporting shall not apply.

5. Fair delivery – the feet

For a delivery to be fair in respect of the feet, in the delivery stride
(i) the bowler's back foot must land within and not touching the return crease
(ii) the bowler's front foot must land with some part of the foot, whether grounded or raised, behind the popping crease.
If the umpire at the bowler's end is not satisfied that both these conditions have been met, he shall call and signal No ball.

6. Ball bouncing more than twice or rolling along the ground

The umpire at the bowler's end shall call and signal No ball if a ball which he considers to have been delivered, without having previously touched the bat or person of the striker, either
(i) bounces more than twice, or
(ii) rolls along the ground,
before it reaches the popping crease.

7. Ball coming to rest in front of striker's wicket

If a ball delivered by the bowler comes to rest in front of the line of the striker's wicket, without having touched the bat or person of the striker, the umpire shall call and signal No ball and immediately call and signal Dead ball.

8. Call of No ball for infringement of other Laws

In addition to the instances above, an umpire shall call and signal No ball as required by the following Laws:
Law 40.3 – Position of wicket-keeper
Law 41.5 – Limitation of on side fielders
Law 41.6 – Fielders not to encroach on the pitch
Law 42.6 – Dangerous and unfair bowling
Law 42.7 – Dangerous and unfair bowling – action by the umpire
Law 42.8 – Deliberate bowling of high full pitched balls

9. Revoking a call of No ball

An umpire shall revoke the call of No ball if the ball does not leave the bowler's hand for any reason.

10. No ball to over-ride Wide

A call of No ball shall over-ride the call of Wide ball at any time. *See* Law 25.1 (Judging a Wide) and 25.3 (Call and signal of Wide ball).

11. Ball not dead

The ball does not become dead on the call of No ball.

12. Penalty for a No ball

A penalty of one run shall be awarded instantly on the call of No ball. Unless the call is revoked, this penalty shall stand even if a batsman is dismissed. It shall be in addition to any other runs scored, any boundary allowance and any other penalties awarded.

13. Runs resulting from a No ball – how scored

The one run penalty for a No ball shall be scored as a No ball extra. If other penalty runs have been awarded to either side, these shall be scored as in Law 42.17 (Penalty runs). Any runs completed by the batsmen or a boundary allowance shall be credited to the striker if the ball has been struck by the bat; otherwise they also shall be scored as No ball extras.

Apart from any award of a 5 run penalty, all runs resulting from a No ball, whether as No ball extras or credited to the striker, shall be debited against the bowler.

14. No ball not to count
A No ball shall not count as one of the over. *See* Law 22.4 (Balls not to count in the over).

15. Out from a No ball
When No ball has been called, neither batsman shall be out under any of the Laws except 33 (Handled the ball), 34 (Hit the ball twice), 37 (Obstructing the field) or 38 (Run out).

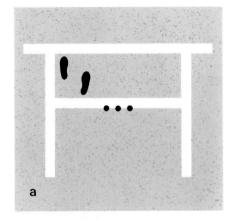

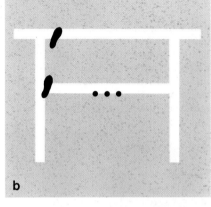

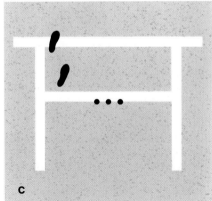

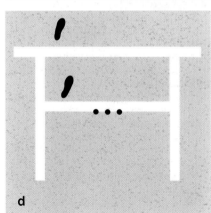

▶ *Fig. 4 The no ball: (a) fair delivery; (b) no ball – back foot is touching return crease; (c) fair delivery; (d) no ball – front foot is over popping crease*

Law 25 – wide ball

1. Judging a Wide
a If the bowler bowls a ball, not being a No ball, the umpire shall adjudge it a Wide if according to the definition in b below, in his opinion, the ball passes wide of the striker where he is standing and would also have passed wide of him standing in a normal guard position.
b The ball will be considered as passing wide of the striker unless it is sufficiently within his reach for him to be able to hit it with his bat by means of a normal cricket stroke.

2. Delivery not a Wide
The umpire shall not adjudge a delivery as being a Wide:
a if the striker, by moving, either
(i) causes the ball to pass wide of him, as defined in **1b** above, or
(ii) brings the ball sufficiently within his reach to be able to hit it with his bat by means of a normal cricket stroke.
b if the ball touches the striker's bat or person.

3. Call and signal of Wide ball
a If the umpire adjudges a delivery to be a Wide he shall call and signal Wide ball as soon as the ball passes the striker's wicket. It shall, however, be considered to have been a Wide from the instant of delivery, even though it cannot be called Wide until it passes the striker's wicket.
b The umpire shall revoke the call of Wide ball if there is then any contact between the ball and the striker's bat or person.
c The umpire shall revoke the call of Wide ball if a delivery is called a No ball. *See* Law 24.10 (No ball to over-ride Wide).

4. Ball not dead
The ball does not become dead on the call of Wide ball.

5. Penalty for a Wide
A penalty of one run shall be awarded instantly on the call of Wide ball. Unless the call is revoked (*see* **3** above), this penalty shall stand even if a batsman is dismissed, and shall be in addition to any other runs scored, any boundary allowance and any other penalties awarded.

6. Runs resulting from a Wide – how scored
All runs completed by the batsmen or a boundary allowance, together with the penalty for the Wide, shall be scored as Wide balls. Apart from any award of a 5 run penalty, all runs resulting from a Wide ball shall be debited against the bowler.

7. Wide not to count
A Wide shall not count as one of the over. *See* Law 22.4 (Balls not to count in the over).

8. Out from a Wide
When Wide ball has been called, neither batsman shall be out under any of the Laws except 33 (Handled the ball), 35 (Hit wicket), 37 (Obstructing the field), 38 (Run out) or 39 (Stumped).

Law 26 – bye and leg bye

1. Byes
If the ball, not being a No ball or a Wide, passes the striker without touching his bat or person, any runs completed by the batsmen or a boundary allowance shall be credited as Byes to the batting side.

2. Leg byes
a If a ball delivered by the bowler first strikes the person of the striker, runs shall be scored only if the umpire is satisfied that the striker has:
either: attempted to play the ball with his bat;
or: tried to avoid being hit by the ball.

If the umpire is satisfied that either of these conditions has been met, and the ball makes no subsequent contact with the bat, runs completed by the batsmen or a boundary allowance shall be credited to the batting side as in (b). Note, however, the provisions of Laws 34.3 (Ball lawfully struck more than once) and 34.4 (Runs permitted from ball lawfully struck more than once).

b The runs in (a) above shall

(i) if the delivery is not a No ball, be scored as Leg byes

(ii) if No ball has been called, be scored together with the penalty for the No ball as No ball extras.

3. Leg byes not to be awarded

If in the circumstances of **2a** above, the umpire considers that neither of the conditions (i) and (ii) has been met, then Leg byes will not be awarded. The batting side shall not be credited with any runs from that delivery apart from the one run penalty for a No ball if applicable. Moreover, no other penalties shall be awarded to the batting side when the ball is dead. *See* Law 42.17 (Penalty runs). The following procedure shall be adopted.

a If no run is attempted but the ball reaches the boundary, the umpire shall call and signal Dead ball, and disallow the boundary.

b If runs are attempted and if:

(i) neither batsman is dismissed and the ball does not become dead for any other reason, the umpire shall call and signal Dead ball as soon as one run is completed or the ball reaches the boundary. The batsmen shall return to their original ends. The run or boundary shall be disallowed

(ii) before one run is completed or the ball reaches the boundary, a batsman is dismissed, or the ball becomes dead for any other reason, all the provisions of the Laws will apply, except that no runs and no penalties shall be credited to the batting side, other than the penalty for a No ball if applicable.

Law 27 – Appeals

1. Umpire not to give batsman out without an appeal

Neither umpire shall give a batsman out, even though he may be out under the Laws, unless appealed to by the fielding side. This shall not debar a batsman who is out under any of the Laws from leaving his wicket without an appeal having been made. Note, however, the provisions of **7** below.

2. Batsman dismissed

A batsman is dismissed if, either

a he is given out by an umpire, on appeal, or

b he is out under any of the Laws and leaves his wicket as in **1** above.

3. Timing of appeals

For an appeal to be valid it must be made before the bowler begins his run up or, if he has no run up, his bowling action to deliver the next ball, and before Time has been called.

The call of Over does not invalidate an appeal made prior to the start of the following over provided Time has not been called. *See* Laws 16.2 (Call of Time) and 22.2 (Start of an over).

4. Appeal 'How's That?'

An appeal "How's That?" covers all ways of being out.

5. Answering appeals

The umpire at the bowler's end shall answer all appeals except those arising out of any of Laws 35 (Hit wicket), 39 (Stumped) or 38 (Run out) when this occurs at the striker's wicket. A decision Not out by one umpire shall not prevent the other umpire from giving a decision, provided that each is considering only matters within his jurisdiction.

When a batsman has been given Not out, either umpire may, within his jurisdiction, answer a further appeal provided that it is made in accordance with **3** above.

6. Consultation by umpires

Each umpire shall answer appeals on matters within his own jurisdiction. If an umpire is doubtful about any point that the other umpire may have been in a better position to see, he shall consult the latter on this point of fact and shall then give his decision. If, after consultation, there is still doubt remaining the decision shall be Not out.

7. Batsman leaving his wicket under a misapprehension

An umpire shall intervene if satisfied that a batsman, not having been given out, has left his wicket under a misapprehension that he is out. The umpire intervening shall call and signal Dead ball to prevent any further action by the fielding side and shall recall the batsman.

8. Withdrawal of an appeal

The captain of the fielding side may withdraw an appeal only with the consent of the umpire within whose jurisdiction the appeal falls and before the outgoing batsman has left the field of play. If such consent is given the umpire concerned shall, if applicable, revoke his decision and recall the batsman.

9. Umpire's decision
An umpire may alter his decision provided that such alteration is made promptly. This apart, an umpire's decision, once made, is final.

Law 28 – the wicket is down

1. Wicket put down
a The wicket is put down if a bail is completely removed from the top of the stumps, or a stump is struck out of the ground by:
(i) the ball
(ii) the striker's bat, whether he is holding it or has let go of it
(iii) the striker's person or by any part of his clothing or equipment becoming detached from his person
(iv) a fielder, with his hand or arm, providing that the ball is held in the hand or hands so used, or in the hand of the arm so used.
The wicket is also put down if a fielder pulls a stump out of the ground in the same manner.
b The disturbance of a bail, whether temporary or not, shall not constitute its complete removal from the top of the stumps, but if a bail in falling lodges between two of the stumps this shall be regarded as complete removal.

2. One bail off
If one bail is off, it shall be sufficient for the purpose of putting the wicket down to remove the remaining bail, or to strike or pull any of the three stumps out of the ground, in any of the ways stated in **1** above.

3. Remaking the wicket
If the wicket is broken or put down while the ball is in play, the umpire shall not remake the wicket until the ball is dead. *See* Law 23 (Dead ball). Any fielder, however, may:
(i) replace a bail or bails on top of the stumps
(ii) put back one or more stumps into the ground where the wicket originally stood.

4. Dispensing with bails
If the umpires have agreed to dispense with bails, in accordance with Law 8.5 (Dispensing with bails), the decision as to whether the wicket has been put down is one for the umpire concerned to decide.
a After a decision to play without bails, the wicket has been put down if the umpire concerned is satisfied that the wicket has been struck by the ball, by the striker's bat, person, or items of his clothing or equipment separated from his person as described in **1**a(ii) or **1**a(iii) above, or by a fielder with the hand holding the ball or with the arm of the hand holding the ball.
b If the wicket has already been broken or put down, **a** above shall apply to any stump or stumps still in the ground. Any fielder may replace a stump or stumps, in accordance with **3** above, in order to have an opportunity of putting the wicket down.

Law 29 – batsman out of his ground

1. When out of his ground
A batsman shall be considered to be out of his ground unless his bat or some part of his person is grounded behind the popping crease at that end.

2. Which is a batsman's ground
a If only one batsman is within a ground
(i) it is his ground
(ii) it remains his ground even if he is later joined there by the other batsman.
b If both batsmen are in the same ground and one of them subsequently leaves it, **a**(i) above applies.

c If there is no batsman in either ground, then each ground belongs to whichever of the batsmen is nearer to it, or, if the batsmen are level, to whichever was nearer to it immediately prior to their drawing level.
d If a ground belongs to one batsman, then, unless there is a striker with a runner, the other ground belongs to the other batsman irrespective of his position.
e When a batsman with a runner is striker, his ground is always that at the wicket-keeper's end. However, **a**, **b**, **c** and **d** above will still apply, but only to the runner and the non-striker, so that that ground will also belong to either the non-striker or the runner, as the case may be.

3. Position of non-striker

The batsman at the bowler's end should be positioned on the opposite side of the wicket to that from which the ball is being delivered, unless a request to do otherwise is granted by the umpire.

Law 30 – bowled

1. Out bowled

a The striker is out Bowled if his wicket is put down by a ball delivered by the bowler, not being a No ball, even if it first touches his bat or person.

b Notwithstanding **a** above he shall not be out Bowled if before striking the wicket the ball has been in contact with any other player or with an umpire. He will, however, be subject to Laws 33 (Handled the ball), 37 (Obstructing the field), 38 (Run out) and 39 (Stumped).

2. Bowled to take precedence

The striker is out Bowled if his wicket is put down as in **1** above, even though a decision against him for any other method of dismissal would be justified.

Law 31 – timed out

1. Out Timed out

a Unless Time has been called, the incoming batsman must be in position to take guard or for his partner to be ready to receive the next ball within 3 minutes of the fall of the previous wicket. If this requirement is not met, the incoming batsman will be out, Timed out.
b In the event of protracted delay in which no batsman comes to the wicket, the umpires shall adopt the procedure of Law 21.3 (Umpires awarding a match). For the purposes of that Law the start of the action shall be taken as the expiry of the 3 minutes referred to above.

2. Bowler does not get credit

The bowler does not get credit for the wicket.

Law 32 – caught

1. Out Caught

The striker is out Caught if a ball delivered by the bowler, not being a No ball, touches his bat without having previously been in contact with any member of the fielding side and is subsequently held by a fielder as a fair catch before it touches the ground.

2. Caught to take precedence

If the criteria of **1** above are met and the striker is not out Bowled, then he is out Caught, even though a decision against either batsman for another method of dismissal would be justified. Runs completed by the batsmen before the completion of the catch will not be scored. Note also Laws 21.6 (Winning hit or extras) and 42.17**b** (Penalty runs).

3. A fair catch

A catch shall be considered to have been fairly made if:
a throughout the act of making the catch
(i) any fielder in contact with the ball is within the field of play. *See* **4** below

(ii) the ball is at no time in contact with any object grounded beyond the boundary.

The act of making the catch shall start from the time when a fielder first handles the ball and shall end when a fielder obtains complete control both over the ball and over his own movement
b the ball is hugged to the body of the catcher or accidentally lodges in his clothing or, in the case of the wicket-keeper, in his pads. However, it is not a fair catch if the ball lodges in a protective helmet worn by a fielder. *See* Law 23 (Dead ball)
c the ball does not touch the ground, even though the hand holding it does so in effecting the catch
d a fielder catches the ball after it has been lawfully struck more than once by the striker, but only if the ball has not touched the ground since first being struck
e a fielder catches the ball after it has touched an umpire, another fielder or the other batsman. However, it is not a fair catch if the ball has touched a protective helmet worn by a fielder, although the ball remains in play
f a fielder catches the ball in the air after it has crossed the boundary provided that:
(i) he has no part of his person touching, or grounded beyond, the boundary at any

time when he is in contact with the ball
(ii) the ball has not been grounded beyond the boundary.
See Law 19.3 (Scoring a boundary)
g the ball is caught off an obstruction within the boundary, provided it has not previously been decided to regard the obstruction as a boundary.

4. Fielder within the field of play

a A fielder is not within the field of play if he touches the boundary or has any part of his person grounded beyond the boundary. *See* Law 19.3 (Scoring a boundary).
b 6 runs shall be scored if a fielder:
(i) has any part of his person touching, or grounded beyond, the boundary when he catches the ball
(ii) catches the ball and subsequently touches the boundary or grounds some part of his person over the boundary while carrying the ball but before completing the catch

See Laws 19.3 (Scoring a boundary) and 19.4 (Runs allowed for boundaries).

5. No runs to be scored

If the striker is dismissed Caught, runs from that delivery completed by the batsmen before the completion of the catch shall not be scored, but any penalties awarded to either side when the ball is dead, if applicable, will stand. Law 18.12a (Batsman returning to wicket he has left) shall apply from the instant of the catch.

Law 33 – handled the ball

1. Out Handled the ball
Either batsman is out Handled the ball if he wilfully touches the ball while in play with a hand or hands not holding the bat unless he does so with the consent of the opposing side.

2. Not out Handled the ball
Notwithstanding **1** above, a batsman will not be out under this Law if:
(i) he handles the ball in order to avoid injury
(ii) he uses his hand or hands to return the ball to any member of the fielding side without the consent of that side. Note, however, the provisions of Law 37.4 (Returning the ball to a member of the fielding side).

3. Runs scored
If either batsman is dismissed under this Law, any runs completed before the offence, together with any penalty extras and the penalty for a No ball or Wide, if applicable, shall be scored. *See* Laws 18.10 (Runs scored when a batsman is dismissed) and 42.17 (Penalty runs).

4. Bowler does not get credit
The bowler does not get credit for the wicket.

Law 34 – hit the ball twice

1. Out Hit the ball twice
a The striker is out Hit the ball twice if, while the ball is in play, it strikes any part of his person or is struck by his bat and, before the ball has been touched by a fielder, he wilfully strikes it again with his bat or person, other than a hand not holding the bat, except for the sole purpose of guarding his wicket. *See* **3** below and Laws 33 (Handled the ball) and 37 (Obstructing the field).
b For the purpose of this Law, 'struck' or 'strike' shall include contact with the person of the striker.

2. Not out Hit the ball twice
Notwithstanding **1a** above, the striker will not be out under this Law if:
(i) he makes a second or subsequent stroke in order to return the ball to any member of the fielding side. Note, however, the provisions of Law 37.4 (Returning the ball to a member of the fielding side)
(ii) he wilfully strikes the ball after it has touched a fielder. Note, however, the provisions of Law 37.1 (Out Obstructing the field).

3. Ball lawfully struck more than once
Solely in order to guard his wicket and before the ball has been touched by a fielder, the striker may lawfully strike the ball more than once with his bat or with any part of his person other than a hand not holding the bat.

Notwithstanding this provision, the striker may not prevent the ball from being caught by making more than one stroke in defence of his wicket. *See* Law 37.3 (Obstructing a ball from being caught).

4. Runs permitted from ball lawfully struck more than once
When the ball is lawfully struck more than once, as permitted in **3** above, only the first strike is to be considered in determining whether runs are to be allowed and how they are to be scored.
a If on the first strike the umpire is satisfied that, either

(i) the ball first struck the bat, or

(ii) the striker attempted to play the ball with his bat, or

(iii) the striker tried to avoid being hit by the ball then any penalties to the batting side that are applicable shall be allowed.

b If the conditions in **a** above are met then, if they result from overthrows, and only if they result from overthrows, runs completed by the batsmen or a boundary will be allowed in addition to any penalties that are applicable. They shall be credited to the striker if the first strike was with the bat. If the first strike was on the person of the striker they shall be scored as Leg byes or No ball extras, as appropriate. *See* Law 26.2 (Leg byes).

c If the conditions of **a** above are met and there is no overthrow until after the batsmen have started to run, but before one run is completed,

(i) only subsequent completed runs or a boundary shall be allowed. The first run shall count as a completed run for this purpose only if the batsmen have not crossed at the instant of the throw

(ii) if in these circumstances the ball goes to the boundary from the throw then, notwithstanding the provisions of Law 19.6 (Overthrow or wilful act of fielder), only the boundary allowance shall be scored

(iii) if the ball goes to the boundary as the result of a further overthrow, then runs completed by the batsmen after the first throw and before this final throw shall be added to the boundary allowance. The run in progress at the first throw will count only if they have not crossed at that moment; the run in progress at the final throw shall count only if they have crossed at that moment. Law 18.12 (Batsman returning to wicket he has left) shall apply as from the moment of the final throw.

d If, in the opinion of the umpire, none of the conditions in **a** above have been met then, whether there is an overthrow or not, the batting side shall not be credited with any runs from that delivery apart from the penalty for a No ball if applicable. Moreover, no other penalties shall be awarded to the batting side when the ball is dead. *See* Law 42.17 (Penalty runs).

5. Ball lawfully struck more than once – action by the umpire

If no runs are to be allowed, either in the circumstances of **4d** above, or because there has been no overthrow and

a if no run is attempted but the ball reaches the boundary, the umpire shall call and signal Dead ball and disallow the boundary

b if the batsmen run and

(i) neither batsman is dismissed and the ball does not become dead for any other reason, the umpire shall call and signal Dead ball as soon as one run is completed or the ball reaches the boundary. The batsmen shall return to their original ends. The run or boundary shall be disallowed.

(ii) a batsman is dismissed, or if for any other reason the ball becomes dead before one run is completed or the ball reaches the boundary, all the provisions of the Laws will apply except that the award of penalties to the batting side shall be as laid down in **4a** or **4d** above as appropriate.

6. Bowler does not get credit

The bowler does not get credit for the wicket.

Law 35 – hit wicket

1. Out Hit wicket

a The striker is out Hit wicket if, after the bowler has entered his delivery stride and while the ball is in play, his wicket is put down either by the striker's bat or person as described in Law 28.1**a**(ii) and (iii) (Wicket put down), either

(i) in the course of any action taken by him in preparing to receive or in receiving a delivery, or

(ii) in setting off for his first run immediately after playing, or playing at, the ball, or

(iii) if he makes no attempt to play the ball, in setting off for his first run, providing that in the opinion of the umpire this is immediately after he has had the opportunity of playing the ball, or

(iv) in lawfully making a second or further stroke for the purpose of guarding his wicket within the provisions of Law 34.3 (Ball lawfully struck more than once).

b If the striker puts his wicket down in any of the ways described in Law 28.1(a)(ii) and (iii) (Wicket put down) before the bowler has entered his delivery stride, either umpire shall call and signal Dead ball.

2. Not out Hit wicket

Notwithstanding **1** above, the batsman is not out under this Law should his wicket be put down in any of the ways referred to in **1** above if:

a it occurs after he has completed any action in receiving the delivery, other than in **1**(a)(ii), (iii) or (iv) above

b it occurs when he is in the act of running, other than in setting off immediately for his first run

c it occurs when he is trying to avoid being run out or stumped

d it occurs while he is trying to avoid a throw-in at any time

e the bowler, after entering his delivery stride, does not deliver the ball. In this case either umpire shall immediately call and signal Dead ball. *See* Law 23.3 (Umpire calling and signalling Dead ball).

f the delivery is a No ball.

Law 36 – leg before wicket

1. Out LBW

The striker is out LBW in the circumstances set out below.

a The bowler delivers a ball, not being a No ball, and

b the ball, if it is not intercepted full pitch, pitches in line between wicket and wicket or on the off side of the striker's wicket, and

c the ball not having previously touched his bat, the striker intercepts the ball, either full-pitch or after pitching, with any part of his person, and

d the point of impact, even if above the level of the bails, either

(i) is between wicket and wicket, or

(ii) is either between wicket and wicket or outside the line of the off stump, if the striker has made no genuine attempt to play the ball with his bat, and

e but for the interception, the ball would have hit the wicket.

2. Interception of the ball

a In assessing points **c**, **d** and **e** in **1** above, only the first interception is to be considered.

b In assessing point **e** in **1** above, it is to be assumed that the path of the ball before interception would have continued after interception, irrespective of whether the ball might have pitched subsequently or not.

3. Off side of wicket

The off side of the striker's wicket shall be determined by the striker's stance at the moment the ball comes into play for that delivery.

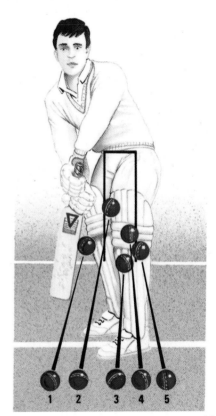

▶ *Fig. 5 LBW: (1) not out – ball not pitching between wicket and wicket and batsman attempting a stroke; (2) and (3) out – if ball not rising to pass over stumps; (4) out – if leg break not enough to make ball pass outside off stump; (5) not out – ball pitching outside line of leg stump*

Law 37 – obstructing the field

1. Out Obstructing the field

Either batsman is out Obstructing the field if he wilfully obstructs or distracts the opposing side by word or action. It shall be regarded as obstruction if either batsman wilfully, and without the consent of the fielding side, strikes the ball with his bat or person, other than a hand not holding the bat, after the ball has touched a fielder. *See* **4** below.

2. Accidental obstruction

It is for either umpire to decide whether any obstruction or distraction is wilful or not. He shall consult the other umpire if he has any doubt.

3. Obstructing a ball from being caught

The striker is out should wilful obstruction or distraction by either batsman prevent a catch being made.

This shall apply even though the striker causes the obstruction in lawfully guarding his wicket under the provisions of Law 34.3 (Ball lawfully struck more than once).

4. Returning the ball to a member of the fielding side

Either batsman is out under this Law if, without the consent of the fielding side and while the ball is in play, he uses his bat or person to return the ball to any member of that side.

5. Runs scored

If a batsman is dismissed under this Law, runs completed by the batsmen before the offence shall be scored, together with the penalty for a No ball or a Wide, if applicable. Other penalties that may be awarded to either side when the ball is dead shall also stand. *See* Law 42.17**b** (Penalty runs).

If, however, the obstruction prevents a catch from being made, runs completed by the batsmen before the offence shall not be scored, but other penalties that may be awarded to either side when the ball is dead shall stand. *See* Law 42.17**b** (Penalty runs).

6. Bowler does not get credit

The bowler does not get credit for the wicket.

Law 38 – run out

1. Out Run out

a Either batsman is out Run out, except as in **2** below, if at any time while the ball is in play:
(i) he is out of his ground, and
(ii) his wicket is fairly put down by the opposing side
b **a** above shall apply even though No ball has been called and whether or not a run is being attempted, except in the circumstances of Law 39.3**b** (Not out Stumped).

2. Batsman not Run out

Notwithstanding **1** above, a batsman is not out Run out if:
a he has been within his ground and has subsequently left it to avoid injury, when the wicket is put down
b the ball has not subsequently been touched again by a fielder, after the bowler has entered his delivery stride, before the wicket is put down
c the ball, having been played by the striker, or having come off his person, directly strikes a helmet worn by a fielder and without further contact with him or any other fielder rebounds directly on to the wicket. However, the ball remains in play and either batsman may be Run out in the

circumstances of **1** above if a wicket is subsequently put down

d he is out Stumped. *See* Law 39.1**b** (Out Stumped)

e he is out of his ground, not attempting a run and his wicket is fairly put down by the wicket-keeper without the intervention of another member of the fielding side, if No ball has been called. *See* Law 39.3**b** (Not out Stumped).

3. Which batsman is out

The batsman out in the circumstances of **1** above is the one whose ground is at the end where the wicket is put down. *See* Laws 2.8 (Transgression of the Laws by a batsman who has a runner) and 29.2 (Which is a batsman's ground).

4. Runs scored

If a batsman is dismissed Run out, the batting side shall score the runs completed before the dismissal, together with the penalty for a No ball or a Wide, if applicable. Other penalties to either side that may be awarded when the ball is dead shall also stand. *See* Law 42.17 (Penalty runs).

If, however, a striker with a runner is himself dismissed Run out, runs completed by the runner and the other batsman before the dismissal shall not be scored.

The penalty for a No ball or a Wide and any other penalties to either side that may be awarded when the ball is dead shall stand. *See* Laws 2.8 (Transgression of the Laws by a batsman who has a runner) and 42.17**b** (Penalty runs).

5. Bowler does not get credit

The bowler does not get credit for the wicket.

Law 39 – stumped

1. Out Stumped

a The striker is out Stumped if
(i) he is out of his ground, and
(ii) he is receiving a ball which is not a No ball, and
(iii) he is not attempting a run, and
(iv) his wicket is put down by the wicket-keeper without the intervention of another member of the fielding side. Note Law 40.3 (Position of wicket-keeper).

b The striker is out Stumped if all the conditions of **a** above are satisfied, even though a decision of Run out would be justified.

2. Ball rebounding from wicket-keeper's person

a If the wicket is put down by the ball, it shall be regarded as having been put down by the wicket-keeper if the ball
(i) rebounds on to the stumps from any part of his person or equipment, other than a protective helmet, or
(ii) has been kicked or thrown on to the stumps by the wicket-keeper.

b If the ball touches a helmet worn by the wicket-keeper, the ball is still in play but the striker shall not be out Stumped. He will, however, be liable to be Run out in these circumstances if there is subsequent contact between the ball and any member of the fielding side. Note, however, **3** below.

3. Not out Stumped

a If the striker is not out Stumped, he is liable to be out Run out if the conditions of Law 38 (Run out) apply, except as set out in **b** below.

b The striker shall not be out Run out if he is out of his ground, not attempting a run, and his wicket is fairly put down by the wicket-keeper without the intervention of another member of the fielding side, if No ball has been called.

Law 40 – the wicket-keeper

1. Protective equipment
The wicket-keeper is the only member of the fielding side permitted to wear gloves and external leg guards. If he does so, these are to be regarded as part of his person for the purposes of Law 41.2 (Fielding the ball). If by his actions and positioning it is apparent to the umpires that he will not be able to discharge his duties as a wicket-keeper, he shall forfeit this right and also the right to be recognised as a wicket-keeper for the purposes of Laws 32.3 (A fair catch), 39 (Stumped), 41.1 (Protective equipment), 41.5 (Limitation of on side fielders) and 41.6 (Fielders not to encroach on the pitch).

2. Gloves
If, as permitted under 1 above, the wicket-keeper wears gloves, they shall have no webbing between fingers except joining index finger and thumb, where webbing may be inserted as a means of support. If used, the webbing shall be
a a single piece of non-stretch material which, although it may have facing material attached, shall have no reinforcement or tucks
b such that the top edge of the webbing

(i) does not protrude beyond the straight line joining the top of the index finger to the top of the thumb
(ii) is taut when a hand wearing the glove has the thumb fully extended.

3. Position of wicket-keeper
The wicket-keeper shall remain wholly behind the wicket at the striker's end from the moment the ball comes into play until
a a ball delivered by the bowler, either
(i) touches the bat or person of the striker, or
(ii) passes the wicket at the striker's end, or
b the striker attempts a run.
In the event of the wicket-keeper contravening this Law, the umpire at the striker's end shall call and signal No ball as soon as possible after the delivery of the ball.

4. Movement by wicket-keeper
It is unfair if a wicket-keeper standing back makes a significant movement towards the wicket after the ball comes into play and before it reaches the striker. In the event of such unfair movement by the wicket-keeper, either umpire shall call and signal Dead ball. It will not be considered a significant movement if the wicket-keeper moves a few paces forward for a slower delivery.

5. Restriction on actions of wicket-keeper
If, in the opinion of either umpire, the wicket-keeper interferes with the striker's right to play the ball and to guard his wicket, Law 23.3(b)(vi) (Umpire calling and signalling Dead ball) shall apply. If, however, the umpire concerned considers that the interference by the wicket-keeper was wilful, then Law 42.4 (Deliberate attempt to distract striker) shall apply.

▲ *Fig, 6 Wicket-keeping gloves*

6. Interference with wicket-keeper by striker

If, in playing at the ball or in the legitimate defence of his wicket, the striker interferes with the wicket-keeper, he shall not be out, except as provided for in Law 37.3 (Obstructing a ball from being caught).

Law 41 – the fielder

1. Protective equipment

No member of the fielding side other than the wicket-keeper shall be permitted to wear gloves or external leg guards. In addition, protection for the hand or fingers may be worn only with the consent of the umpires.

2. Fielding the ball

A fielder may field the ball with any part of his person but if, while the ball is in play he wilfully fields it otherwise,

a the ball shall become dead and 5 penalty runs shall be awarded to the batting side. *See* Law 42.17 (Penalty runs). The ball shall not count as one of the over

b the umpire shall inform the other umpire, the captain of the fielding side, the batsmen and, as soon as practicable, the captain of the batting side of what has occurred

c the umpires together shall report the occurrence as soon as possible to the Executive of the fielding side and any Governing Body responsible for the match who shall take such action as is considered appropriate against the captain and player concerned.

3. Protective helmets belonging to the fielding side

Protective helmets, when not in use by fielders, shall only be placed, if above the surface, on the ground behind the wicket-keeper and in line with both sets of stumps. If a helmet belonging to the fielding side is on the ground within the field of play, and the ball while in play strikes it, the ball shall become dead. Five penalty runs shall then be awarded to the batting side. *See* Laws 18.11 (Runs scored when ball becomes dead) and 42.17 (Penalty runs).

4. Penalty runs not to be awarded

Notwithstanding **2** and **3** above, if from the delivery by the bowler the ball first struck the person of the striker and if, in the opinion of the umpire, the striker, neither

(i) attempted to play the ball with his bat, nor
(ii) tried to avoid being hit by the ball,

then no award of 5 penalty runs shall be made and no other runs or penalties shall be credited to the batting side except the penalty for a No ball if applicable. *See* Law 26.3 (Leg byes not to be awarded).

5. Limitation of on side fielders

At the instant of the bowler's delivery there shall not be more than two fielders, other than the wicket-keeper, behind the popping crease on the on side. A fielder will be considered to be behind the popping crease unless the whole of his person, whether grounded or in the air, is in front of this line.

In the event of infringement of this Law by the fielding side, the umpire at the striker's end shall call and signal No ball.

6. Fielders not to encroach on the pitch

While the ball is in play and until the ball has made contact with the bat or person of the striker, or has passed the striker's bat, no fielder, other than the bowler, may have any part of his person grounded on or extended over the pitch.

In the event of infringement of this Law by any fielder other than the wicket-keeper, the umpire at the bowler's end shall call and signal No ball as soon as possible after the delivery of the ball. Note, however, Law 40.3 (Position of wicket-keeper).

7. Movement by fielders

Any significant movement by any fielder after the ball comes into play and before the ball reaches the striker is unfair. In the event of such unfair movement, either umpire shall call and signal Dead ball. Note also the provisions of Law 42.4 (Deliberate attempt to distract striker).

8. Definition of significant movement

a For close fielders anything other than minor adjustments to stance or position in relation to the striker is significant.

b In the outfield, fielders are permitted to move in towards the striker or striker's wicket, provided that **5** above is not contravened. Anything other than slight movement off line or away from the striker is to be considered significant.

c For restrictions on movement by the wicket-keeper *see* Law 40.4 (Movement by wicket-keeper).

Law 42 – fair and unfair play

1. Fair and unfair play – responsibility of captains

The responsibility lies with the captains for ensuring that play is conducted within the spirit and traditions of the game, as described in The Preamble – The Spirit of Cricket, as well as within the Laws.

2. Fair and unfair play – responsibility of umpires

The umpires shall be the sole judges of fair and unfair play. If either umpire considers an action, not covered by the Laws, to be unfair, he shall intervene without appeal and, if the ball is in play, shall call and signal Dead ball and implement the procedure as set out in **18** below. Otherwise the umpires shall not interfere with the progress of play, except as required to do so by the Laws.

3. The match ball – changing its condition

a Any fielder may:

(i) polish the ball provided that no artificial substance is used and that such polishing wastes no time

(ii) remove mud from the ball under the supervision of the umpire

(iii) dry a wet ball on a towel.

b It is unfair for anyone to rub the ball on the ground for any reason, interfere with any of the seams or the surface of the ball, use any implement, or take any other action whatsoever which is likely to alter the condition of the ball, except as permitted in **a** above.

c The umpires shall make frequent and irregular inspections of the ball.

d In the event of any fielder changing the condition of the ball unfairly, as set out in **b** above, the umpires after consultation shall:

(i) change the ball forthwith. It shall be for the umpires to decide on the replacement ball, which shall, in their opinion, have had wear comparable with that which the previous ball had received immediately prior to the contravention

(ii) inform the batsmen that the ball has been changed

(iii) award 5 penalty runs to the batting side (*See* **17** below)

(iv) inform the captain of the fielding side that the reason for the action was the unfair interference with the ball

(v) inform the captain of the batting side as soon as practicable of what has occurred

(vi) report the occurrence as soon as possible to the Executive of the fielding side

and any Governing Body responsible for the match, who shall take such action as is considered appropriate against the captain and team concerned.

e If there is any further instance of unfairly changing the condition of the ball in that innings, the umpires after consultation shall:

(i) repeat the procedure in **d**(i), (ii) and (iii) above

(ii) inform the captain of the fielding side of the reason for the action taken and direct him to take off forthwith the bowler who delivered the immediately preceding ball. The bowler thus taken off shall not be allowed to bowl again in that innings

(iii) inform the captain of the batting side as soon as practicable of what has occurred

(iv) report this further occurrence as soon as possible to the Executive of the fielding side and any Governing Body responsible for the match, who shall take such action as is considered appropriate against the captain and team concerned.

4. Deliberate attempt to distract striker

It is unfair for any member of the fielding side deliberately to attempt to distract the striker while he is preparing to receive or receiving a delivery.

a If either umpire considers that any action

by a member of the fielding side is such an attempt, at the first instance he shall:

(i) immediately call and signal Dead ball

(ii) warn the captain of the fielding side that the action is unfair and indicate that this is a first and final warning

(iii) inform the other umpire and the batsmen of what has occurred.

Neither batsman shall be dismissed from that delivery and the ball shall not count as one of the over.

b If there is any further such deliberate attempt in that innings, by any member of the fielding side, the procedures, other than warning, as set out in **a** above shall apply. Additionally, the umpire at the bowler's end shall:

(i) award 5 penalty runs to the batting side. (*See* **17** below)

(ii) inform the captain of the fielding side of the reason for this action and, as soon as practicable, inform the captain of the batting side

(iii) report the occurrence, together with the other umpire, as soon as possible to the Executive of the fielding side and any Governing Body responsible for the match, who shall take such action as is considered appropriate against the captain and player or players concerned.

5. Deliberate distraction or obstruction of batsman

In addition to **4** above, it is unfair for any member of the fielding side, by word or action, wilfully to attempt to distract or to obstruct either batsman after the striker has received the ball.

a It is for either one of the umpires to decide whether any distraction or obstruction is wilful or not.

b If either umpire considers that a member of the fielding side has wilfully caused or attempted to cause such a distraction or obstruction he shall:

(i) immediately call and signal Dead ball

(ii)inform the captain of the fielding side and the other umpire of the reason for the call.

Additionally,

(iii) neither batsman shall be dismissed from that delivery

(iv) 5 penalty runs shall be awarded to the batting side. See **17** below. In this instance, the run in progress shall be scored, whether or not the batsmen had crossed at the instant of the call. See Law 18.11 (Runs scored when ball becomes dead)

(v) the umpire at the bowler's end shall inform the captain of the fielding side of the reason for this action and, as soon as practicable, inform the captain of the batting side

(vi) the ball shall not count as one of the over

(vii) the batsmen at the wicket shall decide which of them is to face the next delivery

(vii) the umpires shall report the occurrence as soon as possible to the Executive of the fielding side and any Governing Body responsible for the match, who shall take such action as is considered appropriate against the captain and player or players concerned.

6. Dangerous and unfair bowling

a *Bowling of fast short pitched balls*:

(i) The bowling of fast short pitched balls is dangerous and unfair if the umpire at the bowler's end considers that by their repetition and taking into account their length, height and direction they are likely to inflict physical injury on the striker, irrespective of the protective equipment he may be wearing. The relative skill of the striker shall be taken into consideration.

(ii) Any delivery which, after pitching, passes or would have passed over head height of the striker standing upright at the crease, although not threatening physical injury, is unfair and shall be considered as part of the repetition sequence in (i) above. The umpire shall call and signal No ball for each such delivery.

b *Bowling of high full pitched balls:*

(i) Any delivery, other than a slow paced one, which passes or would have passed on the full above waist height of the striker standing upright at the crease is to be deemed dangerous and unfair, whether or not it is likely to inflict physical injury on the striker.

(ii) A slow delivery which passes or would have passed on the full above shoulder height of the striker standing upright at the crease is to be deemed dangerous and unfair, whether or not it is likely to inflict physical injury on the striker.

7. Dangerous and unfair bowling – action by the umpire

a As soon as the umpire at the bowler's end decides under **6a** above that the bowling of fast short pitched balls has become dangerous and unfair, or, except as in **8** below, there is an instance of dangerous and unfair bowling as defined in **6b** above, he shall call and signal No ball and, when the ball is dead, caution the bowler, inform the other umpire, the captain of the fielding side and the batsman of what has occurred. This caution shall continue to apply throughout the innings.

b If there is any further instance of dangerous and unfair bowling by the same bowler in the same innings, the umpire at the bowler's

end shall repeat the above procedure and indicate to the bowler that this is a final warning.

Both the above caution and final warning shall continue to apply even though the bowler may later change ends.

c Should there be any further repetition by the same bowler in that innings, the umpire shall:

(i) call and signal No ball

(ii) direct the captain, when the ball is dead, to take the bowler off forthwith. The over shall be completed by another bowler, who shall neither have bowled the previous over nor be allowed to bowl the next over.

The bowler thus taken off shall not be allowed to bowl again in that innings

(iii) report the occurrence to the other umpire, the batsmen and, as soon as practicable, the captain of the batting side

(iv) report the occurrence, with the other umpire, as soon as possible to the Executive of the fielding side and to any Governing Body responsible for the match, who shall take such action as is considered appropriate against the captain and bowler concerned.

8. Deliberate bowling of high, full pitched balls

If the umpire considers that a high full

pitch which is deemed to be dangerous and unfair, as defined in **6b** above, was deliberately bowled then the caution and warning prescribed in **7** above shall be dispensed with. The umpire shall:

a call and signal No ball

b direct the captain, when the ball is dead, to take the bowler off forthwith

c implement the remainder of the procedure as laid down in **7c** above.

9. Time wasting by the fielding side

It is unfair for any member of the fielding side to waste time.

a If the captain of the fielding side wastes time, or allows any member of his side to waste time, or if the progress of an over is unnecessarily slow, at the first instance the umpire shall call and signal Dead ball if necessary and:

(i) warn the captain, and indicate that this is a first and final warning

(ii) inform the other umpire and the batsmen of what has occurred.

b If there is any further waste of time in that innings, by any member of the fielding side, the umpire shall either

(i) if the waste of time is not during the course of an over, award 5 penalty runs to the batting side. *See* **17** below, or

(ii) if the waste of time is during the course

of an over, when the ball is dead, direct the captain to take the bowler off forthwith. If applicable, the over shall be completed by another bowler, who shall neither have bowled the previous over nor be allowed to bowl the next over.

The bowler thus taken off shall not be allowed to bowl again in that innings
(iii) inform the other umpire, the batsmen and, as soon as practicable, the captain of the batting side, of what has occurred
(iv) report the occurrence, with the other umpire, as soon as possible to the Executive of the fielding side and to any Governing Body responsible for the match, who shall take such action as is considered appropriate against the captain and team concerned.

10. Batsman wasting time
It is unfair for a batsman to waste time. In normal circumstances the striker should always be ready to take strike when the bowler is ready to start his run up.
a Should either batsman waste time by failing to meet this requirement, or in any other way, the following procedure shall be adopted. At the first instance, either before the bowler starts his run up or when the ball is dead, as appropriate, the umpire shall:

(i) warn the batsman and indicate that this is a first and final warning. This warning shall continue to apply throughout the innings. The umpire shall so inform each incoming batsman
(ii) inform the other umpire, the other batsman and the captain of the fielding side of what has occurred
(iii) inform the captain of the batting side as soon as practicable.
b if there is any further time wasting by any batsman in that innings, the umpire shall, at the appropriate time while the ball is dead:
(i) award 5 penalty runs to the fielding side. See 17 below
(ii) inform the other umpire, the other batsman, the captain of the fielding side and, as soon as practicable, the captain of the batting side of what has occurred
(iii) report the occurrence, with the other umpire, as soon as possible to the Executive of the batting side and to any Governing Body responsible for the match, who shall take such action as is considered appropriate against the captain and player or players and, if appropriate, the team concerned.

11. Damaging the pitch – area to be protected

a It is incumbent on all players to avoid unnecessary damage to the pitch. It is unfair for any player to cause deliberate damage to the pitch.
b An area of the pitch, to be referred to as 'the protected area', is defined as that area contained within a rectangle bounded at each end by imaginary lines parallel to the popping creases and 5 ft/1.52 m in front of each and on the sides by imaginary lines, one each side of the imaginary line joining the centres of the two middle stumps, each parallel to it and 1 ft/30.48 cm from it.

12. Bowler running on the protected area after delivering the ball
a If the bowler, after delivering the ball, runs on the protected area as defined in 11b above, the umpire shall at the first instance, and when the ball is dead,
(i) caution the bowler. This caution shall continue to apply throughout the innings
(ii) inform the other umpire, the captain of the fielding side and the batsmen of what has occurred.
b If, in that innings, the same bowler runs on the protected area again after delivering the ball, the umpire shall repeat the above procedure, indicating that this is a final warning.
c If, in that innings, the same bowler runs

on the protected area a third time after delivering the ball, when the ball is dead the umpire shall:

(i) direct the captain of the fielding side to take the bowler off forthwith. If applicable, the over shall be completed by another bowler, who shall neither have bowled the previous over nor be allowed to bowl the next over. The bowler thus taken off shall not be allowed to bowl again in that innings

(ii) inform the other umpire, the batsmen and, as soon as practicable, the captain of the batting side of what has occurred

(iii) report the occurrence, with the other umpire, as soon as possible to the Executive of the fielding side and to any Governing Body responsible for the match, who shall take such action as is considered appropriate against the captain and bowler concerned.

13. Fielder damaging the pitch

a If any fielder causes avoidable damage to the pitch, other than as in **12a** above, at the first instance the umpire shall, when the ball is dead,

(i) caution the captain of the fielding side, indicating that this is a first and final warning. This caution shall continue to apply throughout the innings

(ii) inform the other umpire and the batsmen.

b If there is any further avoidable damage to the pitch by any fielder in that innings, the umpire shall, when the ball is dead,

(i) award 5 penalty runs to the batting side. *See* **17** below

(ii) inform the other umpire, the batsmen, the captain of the fielding side and, as soon as practicable, the captain of the batting side of what has occurred

(iii) report the occurrence, with the other umpire, as soon as possible to the Executive of the fielding side and any Governing Body responsible for the match, who shall take such action as is considered appropriate against the captain and player or players concerned.

14. Batsman damaging the pitch

a If either batsman causes avoidable damage to the pitch, at the first instance the umpire shall, when the ball is dead,

(i) caution the batsman. This caution shall continue to apply throughout the innings. The umpire shall so inform each incoming batsman

(ii) inform the other umpire, the other batsman, the captain of the fielding side and, as soon as practicable, the captain of the batting side.

b If there is a second instance of avoidable damage to the pitch by any batsman in that innings

(i) the umpire shall repeat the above procedure, indicating that this is a final warning

(ii) additionally he shall disallow all runs to the batting side from that delivery other than the penalty for a No ball or a Wide, if applicable. The batsmen shall return to their original ends.

c If there is any further avoidable damage to the pitch by any batsman in that innings, the umpire shall, when the ball is dead,

(i) disallow all runs to the batting side from that delivery other than the penalty for a No ball or a Wide, if applicable

(ii) additionally award 5 penalty runs to the fielding side. *See* **17** below

(iii) inform the other umpire, the other batsman, the captain of the fielding side and, as soon as practicable, the captain of the batting side of what has occurred

(iv) report the occurrence, with the other umpire, as soon as possible to the Executive of the batting side and any Governing Body responsible for the match, who shall take such action as is considered appropriate against the captain and player or players concerned.

15. Bowler attempting to run out non-striker before delivery

The bowler is permitted, before entering

his delivery stride, to attempt to run out the non-striker. The ball shall not count in the over.

The umpire shall call and signal Dead ball as soon as possible if the bowler fails in the attempt to run out the non-striker.

16. Batsmen stealing a run

It is unfair for the batsmen to attempt to steal a run during the bowler's run up. Unless the bowler attempts to run out either batsman – *see* **15** above and Law 24.4 (Bowler throwing towards striker's end before delivery) – the umpire shall:

(i) call and signal Dead ball as soon as the batsmen cross in any such attempt.

(ii) return the batsmen to their original ends

(iii) award 5 penalty runs to the fielding side. See **17** below

(iv) inform the other umpire, the batsmen, the captain of the fielding side and, as soon as practicable, the captain of the batting side of the reason for the action taken

(v) report the occurrence, with the other umpire, as soon as possible to the Executive of the batting side and any Governing Body responsible for the match, who shall take such action as is considered appropriate against the captain and player or players concerned.

17. Penalty runs

a When penalty runs are awarded to either side, when the ball is dead the umpire shall signal the penalty runs to the scorers as laid down in Law 3.14 (Signals).

b Notwithstanding the provisions of Law 21.6 (Winning hit or extras), penalty runs shall be awarded in each case where the Laws require the award. Note, however, that the restrictions on awarding penalty runs in Laws 26.3 (Leg byes not to be awarded), 34.4d (Runs permitted from ball struck lawfully more than once) and Law 41.4 (Penalty runs not to be awarded) will apply.

c When 5 penalty runs are awarded to the batting side, under either Law 2.6 (Player returning without permission) or Law 41 (The fielder) or under **3**, **4**, **5**, **9** or **13** above, then:

(i) they shall be scored as penalty extras and shall be in addition to any other penalties

(ii) they shall not be regarded as runs scored from either the immediately preceding delivery or the following delivery, and shall be in addition to any runs from those deliveries

(iii) the batsmen shall not change ends solely by reason of the 5 run penalty.

d When 5 penalty runs are awarded to the fielding side, under Law 18.5b (Deliberate short runs), or under **10**, **14** or **16** above, they shall be added as penalty extras to that side's total of runs in its most recently completed innings. If the fielding side has not completed an innings, the 5 penalty extras shall be added to its next innings.

18. Players' conduct

If there is any breach of the Spirit of the Game by a player failing to comply with the instructions of an umpire, or criticising his decisions by word or action, or showing dissent, or generally behaving in a manner which might bring the game into disrepute, the umpire concerned shall immediately report the matter to the other umpire.

The umpires together shall:

(i) inform the player's captain of the occurrence, instructing the latter to take action

(ii) warn him of the gravity of the offence, and tell him that it will be reported to higher authority

(iii) report the occurrence as soon as possible to the Executive of the player's team and any Governing Body responsible for the match, who shall take such action as is considered appropriate against the captain and player or players, and, if appropriate, the team concerned.

Index

The first entries in each line refer to the page numbers: entries in green are the relevant law

appeal 35–6; 27

bails 14, 37; 8, 28
ball 12, 27, 47, 49, 51–2; 5, 20, 41, 42
   dead 10, 30; 3, 23
   drying the 49; 42
   fast short pitched 50; 42
   handled the 40; 33
   hit twice 40–1; 34
   lost 12, 27; 5, 20
   new 12; 5
   no 10, 31–3; 3, 24
   polishing the 49; 42
   unfit for play 12; 5
   wide 10, 34; 3, 25
bat 13; 6
batsman 5–7, 37–8; 2, 29
   obstructing the field 44; 37
   obstruction of 50; 42
   out of his ground 37–8; 29
boundary 10, 25–7; 3, 19
bowled 38; 30
bye 10, 34; 3, 26

captain 5, 49; 1, 42
catch, fair 39; 32

caught 24, 39; 18, 32
crease 15, 17; 9, 10
   bowling 15; 9
   popping 15; 9
   re-marking the 17; 10
   return 15; 9
cricket, junior 12, 14; 5, 8
   women's 12; 5

declaration 19; 14
delivery, fair 31; 24

field, leaving the 6–7; 2
   obstructing the 24, 44; 18, 37
   practice on the 23; 17
fieldsman 5–7, 47–8; 2, 41
   limitation of on side 47; 41
follow-on 18; 13
foothold 17; 10
forfeiture 19; 14

ground, fitness of 8–9; 3

hole, foot 17; 10
'How's that?' 35; 27

innings 7, 18; 2, 12
interval 19–21; 15
   drinks 20–1; 15
   luncheon 20; 15
   tea 20; 15

leg bye 10, 34–5; 3, 26
light, fitness of 8–9; 3

match, drawn 28; 21
   last hour 21–2; 16
   tied 28; 21

non-striker 38, 53; 29, 42

out 10; 3
   not 10; 3
   run 24, 44–5; 18, 38
   timed 38; 31
outfield, mowing of 16–17; 10
over 21–2, 29; 16, 22
   last 21–2; 16
overthrow 27; 19

pitch 13, 16–17, 52–3; 7, 10, 11, 42
   covering the 17; 11
   damaging the 52–3; 42
   mowing the 16–17; 10
   non-turf 13, 17; 7, 10
   rolling the 16; 10
   sweeping the 16; 10
   watering the 17; 10
pitch, fast high full 50–1; 42
play, cessation of 21–2; 16
   fair 8, 49–54; 3, 42
   start of 21; 16
   unfair 8, 49–54; 3, 42
player 5; 1

result 27–9; 21
run 23–5; 18
   short 10, 23–4; 3, 18
   stealing a 54; 42
runner 5–7; 2
run-up, trial 23; 17

scorer 8, 10–11; 3, 4
scoring 23–5; 18
seam, lifting the 49; 42
signals, umpire's 9–10, 11; 3, 4
stumped 45; 39
stumps 12–14; 8
substitution 5–7; 2

throw 31; 24
time wasting 51–2; 42
toss 18; 12

umpire 7–10, 27–9, 35–6, 49, 51, 54; 3, 21, 27, 42
   change of 7; 3

weather, fitness of 8–9; 3
wicket 8, 13–14; 3, 8
   hit 41–2; 35
   leg before 43; 36
wicket down 37; 28
wicket-keeper 32, 45–6; 24, 39, 40
win 27; 21